Teach Yourself

VISUALLY™
Macs

Visual

by Paul McFedries

WILEY

Wiley Publishing, Inc.

Teach Yourself VISUALLY™ Macs

Published by
Wiley Publishing, Inc.
10475 Crosspoint Boulevard
Indianapolis, IN 46256

www.wiley.com

Published simultaneously in Canada

Library of Congress Control Number: 2008935264

ISBN: 978-0-470-38468-8

Manufactured in the United States of America

10 9 8 7 6 5 4 3 2 1

Trademark Acknowledgments

Contact Us

For general information on our other products and services please contact our Customer Care Department within the U.S. at 800-762-2974, outside the U.S. at 317-572-3993 or fax 317-572-4002.

For technical support please visit www.wiley.com/techsupport.

Wiley Publishing, Inc.

US Sales

Contact Wiley
at (800) 762-2974 or
fax (317) 572-4002.

Praise for Visual Books

"Like a lot of other people, I understand things best when I see them visually. Your books really make learning easy and life more fun."

John T. Frey (Cadillac, MI)

"I have quite a few of your Visual books and have been very pleased with all of them. I love the way the lessons are presented!"

Mary Jane Newman (Yorba Linda, CA)

"I just purchased my third Visual book (my first two are dog-eared now!), and, once again, your product has surpassed my expectations.

Tracey Moore (Memphis, TN)

"I am an avid fan of your Visual books. If I need to learn anything, I just buy one of your books and learn the topic in no time. Wonders! I have even trained my friends to give me Visual books as gifts."

Illona Bergstrom (Aventura, FL)

"Thank you for making it so clear. I appreciate it. I will buy many more Visual books."

J.P. Sangdong (North York, Ontario, Canada)

"I have several books from the Visual series and have always found them to be valuable resources."

Stephen P. Miller (Ballston Spa, NY)

"Thank you for the wonderful books you produce. It wasn't until I was an adult that I discovered how I learn – visually. Nothing compares to Visual books. I love the simple layout. I can just grab a book and use it at my computer, lesson by lesson. And I understand the material! You really know the way I think and learn. Thanks so much!"

Stacey Han (Avondale, AZ)

"I absolutely admire your company's work. Your books are terrific. The format is perfect, especially for visual learners like me. Keep them coming!"

Frederick A. Taylor, Jr. (New Port Richey, FL)

"I have several of your Visual books and they are the best I have ever used."

Stanley Clark (Crawfordville, FL)

"I bought my first Teach Yourself VISUALLY book last month. Wow. Now I want to learn everything in this easy format!"

Tom Vial (New York, NY)

"Thank you, thank you, thank you...for making it so easy for me to break into this high-tech world. I now own four of your books. I recommend them to anyone who is a beginner like myself."

Gay O'Donnell (Calgary, Alberta, Canada)

"I write to extend my thanks and appreciation for your books. They are clear, easy to follow, and straight to the point. Keep up the good work! I bought several of your books and they are just right! No regrets! I will always buy your books because they are the best."

Seward Kollie (Dakar, Senegal)

"Compliments to the chef!! Your books are extraordinary! Or, simply put, extra-ordinary, meaning way above the rest! THANK YOU THANK YOU THANK YOU! I buy them for friends, family, and colleagues."

Christine J. Manfrin (Castle Rock, CO)

"What fantastic teaching books you have produced! Congratulations to you and your staff. You deserve the Nobel Prize in Education in the Software category. Thanks for helping me understand computers."

Bruno Tonon (Melbourne, Australia)

"Over time, I have bought a number of your 'Read Less - Learn More' books. For me, they are THE way to learn anything easily. I learn easiest using your method of teaching."

José A. Mazón (Cuba, NY)

"I am an avid purchaser and reader of the Visual series, and they are the greatest computer books I've seen. The Visual books are perfect for people like myself who enjoy the computer, but want to know how to use it more efficiently. Your books have definitely given me a greater understanding of my computer, and have taught me to use it more effectively. Thank you very much for the hard work, effort, and dedication that you put into this series."

Alex Diaz (Las Vegas, NV)

Credits

Project Editor
Sarah Cisco

Sr. Acquisitions Editor
Jody Lefevere

Copy Editor
Scott Tullis

Technical Editor
Dennis Cohen

Editorial Manager
Robyn Siesky

Editorial Assistant
Laura Sinise

Business Manager
Amy Knies

Sr. Marketing Manager
Sandy Smith

Manufacturing
Allan Conley
Linda Cook
Paul Gilchrist
Jennifer Guynn

Book Design
Kathie Rickard

Production Coordinator
Erin Smith

Layout
Elizabeth Brooks
Carrie A. Cesavice
Andrea Hornberger

Screen Artist
Jill A. Proll

Illustrators
Ronda David-Burroughs
Cheryl Grubbs

Proofreader
Melissa D. Buddendeck

Quality Control
John Greenough

Indexer
Broccoli Information Mgt.

Vice President and Executive Group Publisher
Richard Swadley

Vice President and Publisher
Barry Pruett

Composition Director
Debbie Stailey

About the Author

Paul McFedries is a freelance technical writer and passionate Mac fan who has been using Apple computers since 1989. He has written over 50 books that have sold more than three million copies worldwide. These books include the Wiley titles *Macs Portable Genius, MacBook Air Portable Genius*, and *Teach Yourself VISUALLY Computers,* **Fifth Edition**. Please visit Paul's personal website at www.mcfedries.com. Paul is also the proprietor of Word Spy (www.wordspy.com) a website that tracks new words and phrases as they enter the language.

Author's Acknowledgments

All books have text, of course, and I had fun supplying this book with its textual skeleton. However, this book's beauty (and it *is* beautiful, I'm sure you will agree) comes from Wiley's immensely talented group of illustrators, designers, and layout artists. They are all listed in the Credits section on the previous page, and I thank them for creating another gem. The text is important too, and the task of ensuring that what you read here is accurate, logically presented, and free of errors fell to an excellent group of editors that included project editor Sarah Cisco, copy editor Scott Tullis, and technical editor Dennis Cohen. Thanks to all of you for your exceptional competence and hard work. Thanks, as well, to acquistions editor Jody Lefevere for asking me to write this book.

Table of Contents

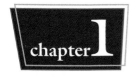

chapter 1 Learning about Mac Types

chapter 2 Understanding What You Can Do with Your Mac

chapter 3   Connecting Devices to Your Mac

chapter 4   Learning Mac Basics

Table of Contents

chapter 5 — Playing and Organizing Music

chapter 6 — Viewing and Editing Your Photos

chapter 7 Creating a Movie

chapter 8 Surfing the World Wide Web

Table of Contents

chapter 11

Working with Your MobileMe Account

chapter 12

Customizing Your Mac

Table of Contents

chapter **15** Troubleshooting Your Mac

How to use this book

How to Use this Teach Yourself VISUALLY Book

Do you look at the pictures in a book or newspaper before anything else on a page? Would you rather see an image instead of read about how to do something? Search no further. This book is for you. Opening *Teach Yourself VISUALLY Macs* allows you to read less and learn more about Macs.

Who Needs This Book

This book is for a reader who has never used a Mac. It is also for more computer literate individuals who want to expand their knowledge of the different features that Macs offer.

Book Organization

Teach Yourself VISUALLY Macs has 15 chapters.

Chapter 1, Learning About Mac Types, introduces you to the Mac and takes you through the various types of Macs that are available.

In Chapter 2, Understanding What You Can Do with Your Mac, you learn about the kinds of tasks you can accomplish with a Mac computer.

Chapter 3, Connecting Devices to Your Mac, shows you how to connect various devices to your Mac, including a printer, modem, iPod, iPhone, and digital camera.

In Chapter 4, Learning Mac Basics, you go through the fundamental techniques that you need to know to use your Mac, including selecting commands, opening and saving documents, and editing text.

Chapter 5, Playing and Organizing Music, teaches you how to work with music on your Mac using the iTunes application.

Chapter 6, Viewing and Editing Your Photos, shows you how to view photos on your Mac, and how to import and edit photos using the iPhoto application.

In Chapter 7, Creating a Movie, you learn how to import video footage into your Mac and then turn that footage into a digital movie complete with transitions, music, titles, and more.

Chapter 8, Surfing the World Wide Web, teaches you the basics of getting around the World Wide Web using Safari, the browser that comes with your Mac.

Chapter 9, Communicating via E-mail and Chat, shows you how to use your Mac's Mail program to set up an e-mail account and to send and receive messages, as well as how to use the iChat application to exchange instant messages.

In Chapter 10, Working with Contacts and Appointments, you learn how to manage your contacts using the Address Book application, and how to track appointments using the iCal application.

Chapter 11, Working with Your MobileMe Account, gives you the basics of logging in and using your MobileMe account.

In Chapter 12, Customizing Your Mac, you find out various ways to personalize your Mac, including changing the desktop background, choosing a screen saver, and customizing the Dock.

Chapter 13, Networking with Your Mac, tells you everything you need to know to connect your Mac to a network and to use the resources on that network.

Chapter 14, Maintaining Your Mac, takes you through a series of tasks designed to help keep your Mac running smoothly and efficiently.

In Chapter 15, Troubleshooting Your Mac, you learn about several of the most common Mac problems and how to solve them.

Chapter Organization

This book consists of sections, all listed in the book's table of contents. A *section* is a set of steps that show you how to complete a specific computer task.

Each section, usually contained on two facing pages, has an introduction to the task at hand, a set of full-color screen shots and steps that walk you through the task, and a set of tips. This format allows you to quickly look at a topic of interest and learn it instantly.

Chapters group together three or more sections with a common theme. A chapter may also contain pages that give you the background information needed to understand the sections in a chapter.

What You Need to Use This Book

The first two chapters of this book give you a general overview of Macs, so they are suitable for someone looking to purchase a Mac. For the rest of the book, you need to have a Mac computer to try out the tasks in each section. Ideally, you should have a recent Mac with an Intel processor, although readers with older

PowerPC-based Macs can still follow along. Your Mac should be running Mac OS X 10.5 (Leopard), although the steps and screen shots for older versions of Mac OS X are similar.

Using the Mouse

This book uses the following conventions to describe the actions you perform when using the mouse:

Click

Press your left mouse button once. You generally click your mouse on something to select something on the screen.

Double-click

Press your left mouse button twice. Double-clicking something on the computer screen generally opens whatever item you have double-clicked.

Right-click

Press your right mouse button if you have a right-click mouse. When you right-click anything on the computer screen, the program displays a shortcut menu containing commands specific to the selected item.

Click and Drag, and Release the Mouse

Move your mouse pointer and hover it over an item on the screen. Press and hold down the left mouse button. Now, move the mouse to where you want to place the item and then release the button. You use this method to move an item from one area of the computer screen to another.

The Conventions in This Book

A number of typographic and layout styles have been used throughout *Teach Yourself VISUALLY Macs* to distinguish different types of information.

Bold

Bold type represents the names of commands and options that you interact with. Bold type also indicates text and numbers that you must type into a dialog box or window.

Italics

Italic words introduce a new term and are followed by a definition.

Numbered Steps

You must perform the instructions in numbered steps in order to successfully complete a section and achieve the final results.

Bulleted Steps

These steps point out various optional features. You do not have to perform these steps; they simply give additional information about a feature.

Indented Text

Indented text tells you what the program does in response to you following a numbered step. For example, if you click a certain menu command, a dialog box may appear, or a window may open. Indented text may also tell you what the final result is when you follow a set of numbered steps.

Notes

Notes give additional information. They may describe special conditions that may occur during an operation. They may warn you of a situation that you want to avoid, for example the loss of data. A note may also cross reference a related area of the book. A cross reference may guide you to another chapter, or another section with the current chapter.

Icons and buttons

Icons and buttons are graphical representations within the text. They show you exactly what you need to click to perform a step.

 You can easily identify the tips in any section by looking for the TIPS icon. Tips offer additional information, including tips, hints, and tricks. You can use the TIPS information to go beyond what you have learn learned in the steps.

Operating System Difference

The text and screen shots in this book are based on Mac OS X 10.5, also known as Leopard. If your Mac uses an earlier version of Mac OS X, such as 10.4 (Tiger) or 10.3 (Panther), then the text and screen shots may be slightly different than what you encounter on your Mac.

Learning about Mac Types

Are you ready to learn about the Mac? This chapter gets you off to a great start by showing you the different types of Macs that are available. You learn about the general Mac types and you learn about the specific Mac models and what features they offer.

Understanding Mac Types

Before you learn about the specific Mac models Apple offers, it is a good idea to take a step back and look at the general types of Macs that are available.

Desktop Macs

A desktop Mac is a Macintosh computer that is designed to sit on your desk. In most cases, you connect the desktop Mac to a separate keyboard, mouse, and monitor. The exception here is the iMac model, which comes with a built-in monitor. Also, the Mac Pro model is quite large, so many people place the system unit on the floor.

Portable Macs

A portable Mac is a Macintosh computer that you can take with you when you leave your home or office. A portable Mac — also called a notebook Mac — comes with a keyboard, mouse, and monitor built in, so it is easy to use in almost any location. A portable Mac also comes with a battery, so you can use it even in places where there is no power outlet available.

PowerPC Macs

From about 1994 to early 2006, all Mac models used a central processing unit (CPU; the "brain" of the computer) called the PowerPC, which was made jointly by IBM and Motorola. Apple no longer uses PowerPC CPUs, but if you are in the market for a used Mac, note that it may come with the PowerPC chip.

Intel Macs

All the current Mac models use a CPU made by Intel Corporation. Apple began the transition from PowerPC to Intel in early 2006, and every Mac made since about August 2006 comes with an Intel CPU. The Intel processors are faster and more reliable than the PowerPC chips, and they use less power, which improves battery life in portable Macs.

Determine the Mac CPU

If you have a Mac and you do not know whether it has an Intel or PowerPC CPU, you can find out. Start your Mac, click the Apple icon in the top-left corner, and then click **About This Mac.** In the About This Mac window that appears, examine the Processor value.

Learn about the iMac

If you are thinking of purchasing an iMac, or just want to know more about this Mac model, this section explains the iMac's features and concepts.

iMac Overview

The iMac is an "all-in-one" computer that combines the system components (the CPU, memory, hard drive, and other internal components) and the screen in a single unit. However, the resulting console is still amazingly thin, so the iMac does not take up very much room on your desk.

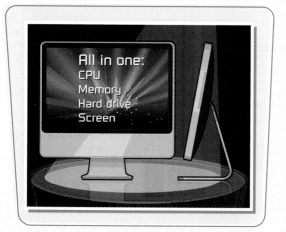

iMac Features

The iMac uses an Intel Core 2 Duo processor, a widescreen display (20 or 24 inches wide), a powerful graphics card, a built-in iSight camera and microphone, wired and wireless networking support, and a CD and DVD burner.

iMac Ports

The back of the iMac has a generous supply of ports that enable you to connect a wide variety of devices.

Audio Out

You use the audio out port to play music or other audio through speakers or headphones.

Audio In

You use the audio in port to bring speech or other audio into the iMac using a microphone, musical instrument, or audio player.

USB

You use the iMac's three USB ports to connect devices that support USB, including keyboards, mice, printers, cameras, external drives, and iPods.

FireWire 400

You use the FireWire 400 port to connect devices that support FireWire 400, including external hard drives, external DVD drives, and video cameras.

Video Out

You use the video out port to connect the iMac to an additional display, such as a second monitor, a TV, or a video projector.

Network

You use the network port to connect the iMac to a wired network.

FireWire 800

You use the FireWire 800 port to connect devices that support FireWire 800, including external hard drives, external DVD drives, and video cameras.

Delve into the Mac Mini

If you are thinking of purchasing a Mac mini, or just want to know more about this Mac model, this section explains the Mac mini's features and concepts.

Mac Mini Overview

The Mac mini is a scaled-down version of a Mac that includes all the standard components — CPU, memory, hard drive, video card, and DVD drive — in a unit that measures only about 6.5 inches square (and about 2 inches tall). This makes the Mac mini perfect for a work area that does not have very much room.

Mac Mini Features

The Mac mini uses an Intel Core 2 Duo processor, an 80GB or 120GB hard drive, wired and wireless networking support, a CD and DVD burner, and numerous ports (see the next page). You need to supply your own keyboard, mouse, and monitor.

Mac Mini Ports

The back of the Mac mini has a number of ports that enable you to connect a wide variety of devices.

Network

You use the network port to connect the Mac mini to a wired network.

FireWire 400

You use the FireWire 400 port to connect devices that support FireWire 400, including external hard drives, external DVD drives, and video cameras.

Video Out

You use the video out port to connect the Mac mini to a computer monitor, TV, or other display.

USB

You use the Mac mini's four USB ports to connect devices that support USB, including keyboards, mice, printers, cameras, external drives, and iPods.

Audio Out

You use the audio out port to play music or other audio through speakers or headphones.

Audio In

You use the audio in port to bring speech or other audio into the Mac mini using a microphone, musical instrument, or audio player.

If you are thinking of purchasing a Mac Pro, or just want to know more about this Mac model, this section explains the Mac Pro's features and concepts.

Mac Pro Overview

The Mac Pro is the fastest and most powerful of all the Mac models. With a fast CPU, lots of memory, a large hard drive, powerful graphics, and a wide variety of expansion options, the Mac Pro is designed for power users who need maximum performance.

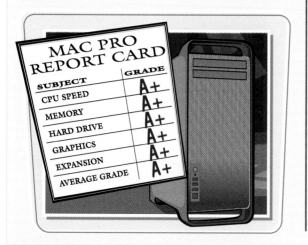

Mac Pro Features

The Mac Pro uses one or two Intel Xeon quad core processors, which gives the Mac Pro the power of up to eight individual CPUs. It also comes with 2GB of memory, a 320GB hard drive, wired and wireless networking support, a CD and DVD burner, and numerous ports. You can upgrade the Mac Pro with a faster CPU, more memory, and multiple hard drives.

Mac Pro Ports

The back of the Mac Pro has a number of ports that enable you to connect a wide variety of devices. Note, too, that the Mac Pro also has several ports on the front.

Video Out

You use a video out port to connect the Mac Pro to a computer monitor, TV, or other display.

USB

You use the Mac Pro's three USB ports to connect devices that support USB, including keyboards, mice, printers, cameras, external drives, and iPods.

FireWire 400

You use the FireWire 400 port to connect devices that support FireWire 400, including external hard drives, external DVD drives, and video cameras.

FireWire 800

You use the FireWire 800 port to connect devices that support FireWire 800, including external hard drives, external DVD drives, and video cameras.

Optical Audio In

You use the optical audio in port to bring digital audio into the Mac Pro using digital audio devices that support optical connections.

Optical Audio Out

You use the optical audio out port to send digital audio from the Mac Pro to digital audio devices that support optical connections.

Network

You use a network port to connect the Mac Pro to a wired network.

Audio Out

You use the audio out port to play music or other audio through speakers or headphones.

Audio In

You use the audio in port to bring speech or other audio into the Mac Pro using a microphone, musical instrument, or audio player.

If you are thinking of purchasing a MacBook Pro, or just want to know more about this Mac model, this section explains the MacBook Pro's features and concepts.

MacBook Pro Overview

The MacBook Pro is a portable computer that combines the monitor and keyboard into a single unit. Instead of a mouse, the MacBook Pro uses a trackpad where you move the pointer by sliding your finger along the pad. The latest MacBook Pro models use multi-touch trackpads, where you use gestures to scroll, rotate, and zoom screen objects.

MacBook Pro Features

The MacBook Pro uses an Intel Core 2 Duo processor, a widescreen display (15.4 or 17 inches measured diagonally), 2GB of memory, a 200GB or 250GB hard drive, a built-in iSight camera and microphone, wired and wireless networking support, and a CD and DVD burner.

• Intel Core 2 Duo processor
• Widescreen display
• 2GB of memory
• 200GB or 250GB hard drive
• iSight camera and microphone
• Wire & wireless network support
• CD & DVD burner

MacBook Pro Ports

The sides of the MacBook Pro have a number of ports that enable you to connect a wide variety of devices.

USB

You use the MacBook Pro's USB ports to connect devices that support USB, including keyboards, mice, printers, cameras, external drives, and iPods.

FireWire 400

You use the FireWire 400 port to connect devices that support FireWire 400, including external hard drives, external DVD drives, and video cameras.

FireWire 800

You use the FireWire 800 port to connect devices that support FireWire 800, including external hard drives, external DVD drives, and video cameras.

Audio Out

You use the audio out port to play music or other audio through speakers or headphones.

Audio In

You use the audio in port to bring speech or other audio into the MacBook Pro using a microphone, musical instrument, or audio player.

Video Out

You use the video out port to connect the MacBook Pro to an additional display, such as a second monitor, a TV, or a video projector.

Network

You use the network port to connect the MacBook Pro to a wired network.

Tour the MacBook Air

If you are thinking of purchasing a MacBook Air, or just want to know more about this Mac model, this section explains the MacBook Air's features and concepts.

MacBook Air Overview

The MacBook Air is a portable computer that combines the monitor and keyboard into a single unit. Instead of a mouse, the MacBook Air uses a multi-touch trackpad where you move the pointer by sliding your finger along the pad, and where you use gestures to scroll, rotate, and zoom screen objects. With a height of just 0.76 inches, the MacBook Air is the world's thinnest notebook computer.

MacBook Air Features

The MacBook Air uses an Intel Core 2 Duo processor, a 13.3-inch widescreen display (measured diagonally), 2GB of memory, an 80GB hard drive, a built-in iSight camera and microphone, and wireless networking support. Note that the MacBook Air does *not* come with wired networking support or a CD or DVD drive.

MacBook Air News!
FEATURES:
Intel Core 2 Duo processor
13.3 - inch widescreen display
2GB of memory
80GB hard drive
iSight camera & microphone
Wireless network support

MacBook Air Ports

The sides of the MacBook Air have a number of ports that enable you to connect a wide variety of devices.

Audio Out

You use the audio out port to play music or other audio through speakers or headphones.

Video Out

You use the video out port to connect the MacBook Air to an additional display, such as a second monitor, a TV, or a video projector.

USB

You use the MacBook Air's USB port to connect a device that supports USB, including a keyboard, mouse, printer, camera, external drive, and iPod.

MacBook Air Accessories

MacBook Air SuperDrive

The MacBook Air does not come with a built-in CD or DVD drive, but you can attach the external MacBook Air SuperDrive to the USB port. The MacBook Air SuperDrive can read and write DVDs and CDs, and weighs just 0.71 pounds.

USB Ethernet Adapter

The MacBook Air does not offer a port for a wired network connection. If you need a faster network connection than the MacBook Air's built-in wireless networking, or if your local network offers only wired connections, you can attach the USB Network Adapter to the computer's USB port.

Take a Look at the MacBook

If you are thinking of purchasing a MacBook, or just want to know more about this Mac model, this section explains the MacBook's features and concepts.

MacBook Overview

The MacBook is a portable computer that combines the monitor and keyboard into a single unit. Instead of a mouse, the MacBook uses a trackpad where you move the pointer by sliding your finger along the pad.

MacBook Features

The MacBook uses an Intel Core 2 Duo processor, a 13.3-inch widescreen display (measured diagonally), 1GB or 2GB of memory, a 120GB or 160GB hard drive, a built-in iSight camera and microphone, wired and wireless networking support, and a CD and DVD burner.

MacBook Features
Intel Core 2 Duo processor
iSight camera & microphone
13.3" widescreen display
1GB or 2GB of memory
120GB or 160GB hard drive
CD & DVD burner
Wired & wireless network support

MacBook Ports

The sides of the MacBook have a number of ports that enable you to connect a wide variety of devices.

Network

You use the network port to connect the MacBook to a wired network.

Video Out

You use the video out port to connect the MacBook to an additional display, such as a second monitor, a TV, or a video projector.

FireWire 400

You use the FireWire 400 port to connect devices that support FireWire 400, including external hard drives, external DVD drives, and video cameras.

USB

You use the MacBook's USB ports to connect devices that support USB, including keyboards, mice, printers, cameras, external drives, and iPods.

Audio Out

You use the audio out port to play music or other audio through speakers or headphones.

Audio In

You use the audio in port to bring speech or other audio into the MacBook using a microphone, musical instrument, or audio player.

Understanding What You Can Do with Your Mac

Are you ready to learn about what you can do with a Mac? In this chapter you find out about the wide variety of tasks you can perform with your Mac, including creating documents, playing music, organizing photos, contacts, and appointments, surfing the Web, and communicating with others.

Create Documents

You can use your Mac to create a wide variety of documents, including lists, letters, memos, budgets, forecasts, presentations, and Web pages.

Text Documents

You can use text-editing software on your Mac to create simple documents such as lists, notes, instructions, and other items that do not require fonts, colors, or other types of formatting. On your Mac, you can use the TextEdit application to create plain text documents, and the Stickies application to create electronic sticky notes.

Word-Processing Documents

You can use word-processing software on your Mac to create letters, résumés, memos, reports, newsletters, brochures, business cards, menus, flyers, invitations, and certificates. Anything that you use to communicate on paper, you can create using your Mac. On your Mac, you can also use TextEdit to create formatted documents. Other examples include Microsoft Word for the Mac and Apple iWork Pages.

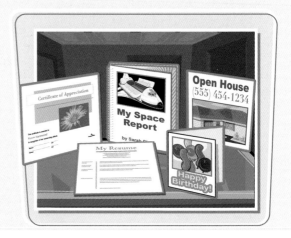

Spreadsheets

A spreadsheet is a software program that enables you to manipulate numbers and formulas to quickly create powerful mathematical, financial, and statistical models. Your Mac comes with a test-drive version of the Apple iWork Numbers application. Another example is Microsoft Excel for the Mac.

Presentations

A presentation program enables you to build professional-looking slides that you can use to convey your ideas to other people. Your Mac comes with a test-drive version of the Apple iWork Keynote application. Another example is Microsoft PowerPoint for the Mac.

Web Pages

You can use Web page-editing software on your Mac to create your own pages to publish to the Web. You can create a personal home page, a blog, or pages to support your business. On your Mac, you can use the iWeb application to create and publish entire Web sites.

Play and Record Music

Your Mac is a veritable music machine that you can use to organize and play your digital music collection. You can rip music from audio CDs, purchase music online, and even record new tunes.

iTunes

Your Mac comes with the iTunes application, which stores your library of digital music files. With iTunes you can play albums and songs, organize tunes into related playlists, download and edit track information, and organize your music to suit your style. You can also use iTunes to listen to Internet-based radio stations.

iTunes Store

You can use the iTunes application to connect directly to the online iTunes store, where you can purchase individual songs, usually for 99 cents per song, or entire albums, usually for $9.99 per album. Your Mac downloads the purchased music to your iTunes library, and you can listen to the music on your Mac or add the music to your iPod.

Import Music from a CD

You can add tracks from a music CD to the iTunes library. This enables you to listen to an album without having to put the CD into your CD or DVD drive each time. In iTunes, the process of copying tracks from a CD to your Mac is called *importing* or *ripping*.

Burn Music to a CD

You can copy, or *burn*, music files from your Mac onto a CD. Burning CDs is a great way to create customized CDs that you can listen to on the computer or in a portable device. You can burn music files using the iTunes application or using the GarageBand application.

Record Music

Your Mac comes with an application called GarageBand that enables you to record your own tunes. You can attach an instrument such as a guitar or keyboard to your Mac and record your playing. You can also use GarageBand to add accompanying instruments such as drums, bass, piano, or another guitar.

Synchronize with an iPod

You can use the iTunes application to copy some or all of your music library to an iPod, which enables you to play your music while you are walking around or on another audio device that connects to the iPod. When you attach the iPod to your Mac using a USB cable, iTunes automatically synchronizes the iPod according to the settings you specify.

View and Organize Your Photos

Your Mac's high-quality display is perfect for displaying, organizing, and editing your digital photos. You can view photo slideshows, import images from a camera, take snapshots, and edit your photos.

View Photos

Your Mac gives you many ways to view your digital photos. If you have Mac OS X 10.5 (Leopard), you can view photos within Finder using the Cover Flow view, or by selecting the photos and pressing Spacebar. You can also double-click a photo file to open it using the Preview application, or you can open a file using the iPhoto application. Also, both Preview and iPhoto enable you to run photo slideshows.

Organize Photos

You can use iPhoto to organize your Mac's collection of digital photos. For example, you can create albums of related photos, and you can create folders in which to store photos. You can also rename and rate photos, apply keywords to photos, flag important photos, and sort photos in various ways.

Import Photos to Your Mac

If you have a digital camera attached to your Mac, you can use either the Image Capture application or the iPhoto application to import some or all of the camera's images to your Mac.

Take Snapshots

If your Mac includes an iSight camera or has a digital video camera connected, you can use the Photo Booth application to take snapshots of whatever subject is currently displayed in the camera. You can also apply various effects to the photos.

Edit Photos

You can use the iPhoto application to edit your digital photos. You can rotate, crop, or straighten a photo; you can modify a photo's exposure, contrast, and sharpness; you can fix problems such as red eye and blemishes; and you can add special effects to a photo.

Play and Make a Movie or DVD

Your Mac's solid graphical underpinnings mean that it is a great tool for playing digital movies and DVDs. You can also use your Mac to create your own digital movies and your own DVDs.

Play a DVD

If your Mac has a DVD drive, you can use the DVD Player application to play a DVD movie. You can either watch the movie in a window while you work on other things, or you can switch to full-screen mode and watch the movie using the entire screen. DVD Player has features that enable you to control the movie playback and volume.

Play a Video File

Your Mac comes with an application called QuickTime Player that can play digital video files. The basic version that comes with your Mac enables you to open video files and control the playback and volume. QuickTime Pro — which you can purchase for $29.99 — adds many extra features, including the ability to record movies and audio and to cut and paste scenes.

Play a Movie, TV Show, or Podcast

You most often use iTunes to play music, but you can also use it to play video files stored on your Mac, movies, and TV shows that you purchase from the iTunes store, as well as podcasts that you download from the iTunes store or subscribe to online.

Make a Movie

Your Mac comes with an application called iMovie that enables you to make your own digital movies. You can import clips from a video camera or video file, add clips to the movie, and rearrange and trim those clips as needed. You can also add transitions between scenes, music and sound effects, titles, and more.

Make a DVD

You can use your Mac to create your own custom DVD discs. Using the iDVD application, you can create a DVD project that includes video footage, photos, and audio effects. You can enhance the project with a custom menu, titles, and sophisticated background and text themes. When you are done, you can burn the project to a DVD disc.

Take Advantage of the Web

You can use your Mac to connect to the Internet and access the Web to look for information or news, buy and sell goods, socialize with others, and more.

Surf the Web

Your Mac comes with a browser application called Safari that you use to surf the Web. With Safari you can navigate Web pages, save favorite Web pages as bookmarks, and view multiple pages in a single window using tabs.

Search for Information

If you need information on a specific topic, free Web sites called *search engines* enable you to quickly search the Web for pages that have the information you require. You can search the Web either by going directly to a search engine site or by using the search feature built into Safari.

Read News

The Web is home to many sites that enable you to read the latest news. For example, many print sources have Web sites, some magazines exist only online, and there are more recent innovations such as blogs and RSS feeds. Some media sites require that you register to access the articles, but on most sites the registration is free.

Buy and Sell

ECommerce — the online buying and selling of goods and services — is a big part of the Web. You can use Web-based stores to purchase books, theater tickets, and even cars, which gives you the convenience of shopping at home, easily comparing prices and features, and having goods delivered to your door. Many sites also enable you to sell or auction your products or household items.

Socialize

The Web offers many opportunities to socialize, whether you are looking for a friend or a date, or you just want some good conversation. However, it is a good idea to observe some common-sense precautions. For example, arrange to meet new friends in public places, supervise all online socializing done by children, and do not give out personal information to strangers.

Take Advantage of MobileMe

You can use your Mac to set up a Web-based MobileMe account that enables you to perform many activities online, including exchanging e-mail, maintaining contacts, tracking appointments, sharing photos, and storing files online. You can also synchronize data between your Mac and your MobileMe account.

Communicate with Others

You can use your Mac to communicate with other people using online technologies such as e-mail and instant messaging.

Exchange E-mail

E-mail is the Internet system that enables you to electronically exchange messages with other Internet users anywhere in the world. To use e-mail, you must have an e-mail account, which is usually supplied by your ISP. The account gives you an e-mail address to which others can send messages. You then set up that account in your Mac's Mail application.

Exchange E-mail over the Web

You can also set up a Web-based e-mail account. Although you can do this using services such as Hotmail.com and Yahoo.com, many Mac users create MobileMe accounts, which include Web-based e-mail. A Web-based account is convenient because it enables you to send and receive messages from any computer that has access to the Internet.

Exchange Instant Messages

Instant messaging allows you to contact other people who are online, thus enabling you to have a real-time exchange of messages. Communicating in real time means that if you send a message to another person who is online, that message appears on the person's computer right away. If that person sends you a response, it appears on your computer right away. On your Mac, you use the iChat application to exchange instant messages.

Audio Chat

You can also use the iChat program to audio chat with another person. With an audio chat, you speak into a microphone and your voice is sent over the Internet to the other person who hears you through his or her computer's speakers. You also hear that person's voice through your own speakers.

Video Chat

You can also use the iChat program to video chat with someone. With a video chat, your image is captured by a video camera — such as the iSight camera built into many Macs — and a microphone captures your voice, and both the video and audio streams are sent over the Internet to the other person. You can also see and hear the other person on your Mac.

Organize Your Contacts and Appointments

You can use your Mac to help you organize your life. Specifically, your Mac comes with tools that enable you to manage your contacts and schedule your appointments.

Maintain Your Address Book

Your Mac comes with an application called Address Book that enables you to store information about your contacts. For each contact, you can store data such as the person's name, address, telephone number, e-mail address, birthday, and more.

Work with Contacts

You can use your Address Book items to perform many different contact-related tasks. For example, you can use Mail to send a message either to individual contacts or to a contact group, which is an Address Book item that contains multiple contacts. Also, you can use iCal to set up a meeting with a contact.

Schedule an Appointment

You can help organize your life by using your Mac to record your appointments on the date and time they occur. You do this using the iCal application, which uses an electronic calendar to store your appointments. You can even configure iCal to display a reminder before an appointment occurs.

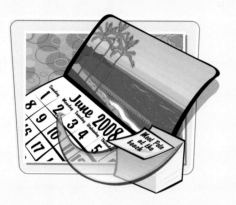

Schedule an All-Day Event

If an appointment has no set time — for example, a birthday, anniversary, or multiple-day event such as a sales meeting or vacation — you can use iCal to set up the appointment as an all-day event.

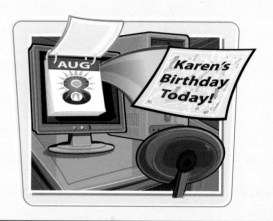

Schedule a Repeating Appointment

If an appointment occurs regularly — for example, once a week or once every three months — you do not need to schedule every appointment by hand. Instead, you can use iCal to configure the activity as a repeating appointment, where you specify the repeat interval. iCal then creates all the future appointments automatically.

Synchronize with MobileMe

If you have a MobileMe account, you can synchronize your Mac's e-mail, contacts, and appointments so that they also appear in the MobileMe's Mail, Contacts, and Calendar applications. If you have a second Mac, you can use MobileMe to keep your e-mail, contacts, and appointments in sync on both Macs.

Connecting Devices to Your Mac

When you plug a device into your Mac, most of the time the device works right away. However, there are some devices that require a bit of extra effort on your part to get them connected and configured. This chapter takes you through a few such devices, including an external display, printer, fax, iPod, iPhone, digital camera, and even another Mac.

Connect Your Mac to an External Display

You can connect your Mac to an external display such as a monitor or a TV. This is essential for machines such as the Mac mini and Mac Pro that do not come with a screen. However, you can also connect an iMac or portable Mac to a larger screen for more viewing area.

The Mac Connection

DVI Port

The Mac Pro, Mac mini, and MacBook Pro use a regular DVI port to output video.

Mini DVI Port

The iMac and MacBook use a Mini DVI port. These Macs come with adapters for connecting to VGA or regular DVI displays.

Micro DVI Port

The MacBook Air uses a Micro DVI port and comes with adapters for connecting to VGA or regular DVI displays.

DVI Port

Most computer monitors come with at least one DVI port, although the configuration (the number of holes) may not match what you have on your Mac. Therefore, the cable you use must have connectors that match the ports on both the Mac and the monitor.

VGA Port

Most computer monitors come with at least one VGA port. To use such a port with your Mac, you need a cable adapter that converts DVI, Mini DVI, or Micro DVI to VGA.

Composite or S-Video Port

Most televisions come with either or both an S-Video port or a composite video port. To use such a port with your Mac, you need a cable adapter that converts DVI, Mini DVI, or Micro DVI to either S-Video or composite video.

Cable Adapters

Macs that use either a Mini DVI port or a Micro DVI port come with adapters that enable you to connect these Macs to VGA or regular DVI displays. You can also purchase from Apple an adapter that enables you to connect your Mac to a composite or S-Video display.

If you have a printer that you want to use to make hard copies of some of your documents, you must first connect the printer to your Mac.

① Connect the printer's USB cable to a free USB port on your Mac, and then turn on the printer.

② Click the Apple icon (🍎).

③ Click **System Preferences.**

Note: *You can also click the System Preferences icon (🖼) in the dock.*

The System Preferences appear.

④ Click **Print & Fax.**

The Print & Fax preferences appear.

● If you see your printer in the Printers list, skip the rest of the steps in this section.

⑤ Click Add (+).

The Printer Browser dialog box appears.

TIP

What do I do if my printer has a parallel port instead of a USB port?
Although almost all new printers come with USB ports, many older printers use a parallel (also called LPT) port instead. No Mac has a corresponding printer port, so you need to purchase a parallel-to-USB adapter cable, which has a parallel connector on one end and a USB connector on the other.

Fortunately, the vast majority of the time your Mac will recognize your printer immediately after you attach it to the USB port, so in most cases you will not need to use the extra steps in this section.

Connect a Printer *(continued)*

6 Click **Default.**

7 In the Printer Name list, click your printer.

8 Use the Name text box to edit the printer name.

9 If the Print Using list shows the wrong printer, click and then click the correct printer.

⓾ Click **Add.**

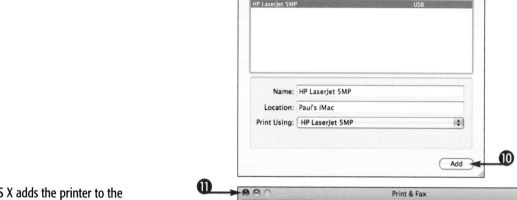

● OS X adds the printer to the Printers list.

⓫ Click **Close** (⬤).

TIPS

What do I do if I do not see my printer in the Print Using list?

First, insert the disc that came with your printer and then run the installation program. If that does not work, follow Steps **1** to **7** and then, in the Print Using list, click ⬍ and then click **Other.** Click the printer disc, locate and choose the printer driver, and then click **Open.**

What if I do not have a printer disc?

If you do not have a printer disc, or if the disc does not contain Mac drivers, visit the printer manufacturer's Web site and download the drivers you need. If you cannot get drivers for the printer (many printer manufacturers do not bother writing Mac drivers), you may still be able to use the printer by choosing **Generic PostScript Printer** in the Print Using list.

Connect a Fax Modem

If you want to send or receive faxes using your Mac, then you must connect an external fax modem, such as Apple's USB Modem.

Some older Macs came with an internal fax modem already installed, so you may not need to connect an external modem.

Connect a Fax Modem

① Connect the fax modem to a free USB port on your Mac.

② Follow Steps **2** to **8** in the previous section to display the Printer Browser dialog box.

③ Click **Fax.**

Note: If you are using a version of OS X earlier than Leopard (10.5), click Default Browser, instead.

④ In the Printer Name list, click your modem.

⑤ Use the Name text box to edit the modem name.

⑥ Click **Add.**

● OS X adds the modem to the Printers list.

⑦ Click **Close** .

What do I do if my modem has a serial port instead of a USB port?

Although almost all new modems come with USB ports, many older modems use a serial port instead. No Mac has a corresponding serial port, so you need to purchase a serial-to-USB adapter or cable, which has a serial connector on one end and a USB connector on the other.

To synchronize some or all of your iTunes library with your iPod, you need to connect the iPod to your Mac.

To connect an iPod you will need the USB cable that came as part of the iPod package.

Connect an iPod

CONNECT THE IPOD

1 Attach the USB connector to a free USB port on your Mac.

2 Attach the other end of the USB cable to the iPod's port.

Your Mac launches iTunes and automatically begins synchronizing the iPod.

DISCONNECT THE IPOD

1 In iTunes, click the eject button (⏏) beside your iPod's name.

iTunes begins releasing the iPod.

Note: See the following Tip to learn when it is safe to disconnect the cable from the iPod.

2 Pinch the sides of the connector and then pull the connector away from the iPod.

3 Disconnect the cable from the Mac's USB port.

Note: If your Mac has two or more free USB ports and you synchronize your iPod frequently, consider leaving the cable plugged into a USB port for easier iPod connections in the future.

TIP

Do I always have to eject my iPod before disconnecting it?

No, not always. You must first eject the iPod if the iPod screen says "Do not disconnect," "Eject Before Disconnecting," or "Sync in Progress." You can safely disconnect the cable from your iPod if the iPod screen says, "OK to disconnect," "Charging," "Charged," or you see the iPod main menu screen.

Connect an iPhone

To synchronize some or all of your iTunes library, Address Book contacts, iCal appointments, Safari bookmarks, and e-mail account settings with your iPhone, you need to connect the iPhone to your Mac.

To connect an iPhone you will need the USB cable and, optionally, the dock that came with the iPhone package.

Connect an iPhone

CONNECT THE IPHONE DIRECTLY

1 Attach the USB connector to a free USB port on your Mac.

2 Attach the other end of the USB cable to the iPhone's port.

Your Mac launches iTunes and automatically begins synchronizing the iPhone.

CONNECT THE IPHONE USING THE DOCK

1 Attach the USB connector to a free USB port on your Mac.

2 Attach the other end of the USB cable to the iPhone dock's port.

3 Insert the iPhone into the dock.

Your Mac launches iTunes and automatically begins synchronizing the iPhone.

TIP

How do I disconnect the iPhone?

First, make sure that the iPhone is not currently synchronizing, in which case it shows "Sync in Progress" on the screen. When the screen says "iPhone sync is complete," you can disconnect the iPhone. In iTunes, click the eject button (⏏) beside your iPhone's name. If you are using the USB cable, pinch the sides of the iPhone connector and then pull the connector away from the iPhone. If you are using the dock, lift the iPhone out of the dock.

Connect an Imaging Device

To import photos from a digital camera, movies from a digital video camera, or images from a scanner, you need to connect the imaging device to your Mac.

Most digital cameras and scanners connect using a USB cable. Most digital video cameras connect using a FireWire cable.

Connect an Imaging Device

① Connect one end of the cable to the imaging device and the other end to your Mac.

Note: If you see either iPhoto (for a digital camera) or iMovie (for a digital video camera), then your Mac has recognized your device and you can skip the rest of these steps.

② Click the Finder icon ( ) in the Dock.

③ Click **Applications.**

④ Double-click **Image Capture.**

The Image Capture application appears.

5 Click **Devices**.

6 Click **Browse Devices**.

Note: You can also press ⌘+B.

7 Click the **Connected** check box beside the imaging device (☐ changes to ☑).

Your Mac launches either iPhoto (for a digital camera) or iMovie (for a digital video camera).

Note: If you are connecting a scanner, be sure to also click the Use TWAIN software check box (☐ changes to ☑).

8 Click .

What is TWAIN software?

TWAIN is a software technology that enables applications such as iPhoto to communicate with a document scanner. (Despite the uppercase letters, TWAIN is not an acronym, although some people jokingly refer to it as Technology Without An Interesting Name.) Your scanner came with a disc that includes the TWAIN software, and you may need to install that software to use your scanner with your Mac.

Why does Image Capture not detect my FireWire digital camcorder?

Most FireWire-compatible digital camcorders are compatible with Macs, but not all. For example, many Sony and JVC digital camcorders do not work with Macs. If you are looking to buy a camcorder, be sure to do some research on the Web to make sure the camcorder you want is Mac-compatible.

Connect a Bluetooth Device

You can make wireless connections to devices such as mice, keyboards, headsets, and cell phones by using the Bluetooth networking technology.

For Bluetooth connections to work, your Mac must support Bluetooth (all newer Macs do) and your device must be Bluetooth-enabled.

Connect a Bluetooth Device

CONNECT A GENERIC BLUETOOTH DEVICE

1 Click the Bluetooth status icon (⁂).

2 Click **Set up Bluetooth Device.**

The Bluetooth Setup Assistant appears.

3 Click **Continue.**

Bluetooth Setup Assistant

Introduction

Welcome to the Bluetooth Setup Assistant.

This computer has Bluetooth wireless capabilities.

The Bluetooth Setup Assistant will walk you through the process of configuring Bluetooth enabled devices for use with this computer.

Go Back   Continue

The Select Device Type dialog box appears.

④ Click the type of Bluetooth device you are going to connect (○ changes to ⦿).

⑤ Click **Continue.**

⑥ Perform whatever steps are necessary to make your Bluetooth device discoverable.

Note: For example, if you are connecting a Bluetooth mouse, the device often has a separate switch or button that makes the mouse discoverable, so you need to turn on that switch or press that button.

● When the Bluetooth Setup Assistant discovers the device, it displays the device name.

⑦ Click **Continue.**

⑧ Perform the steps required to pair your Mac and your device.

Note: See the next two pages for the pairing instructions for a keyboard, headset, and cell phone. A Bluetooth mouse does not require any extra pairing steps.

Your Mac connects with the device.

⑨ Click **Quit.**

 TIPS

What does it mean to make a device "discoverable"?

This means that you configure the device to broadcast that it is available for a Bluetooth connection. Controlling the broadcast is important because you usually want to use a Bluetooth device such as a mouse or keyboard with only a single computer. By controlling when the device is discoverable, you ensure that it works only with the computer you want it to.

What does "pairing" mean?

As a security precaution, many Bluetooth devices do not connect automatically to other devices. This makes sense because otherwise it means a stranger with a Bluetooth device could connect to your cell phone or even your Mac. To prevent this, most Bluetooth devices require you to enter a password before the connection is made. This is known as *pairing* the two devices.

Connect a Bluetooth Device (continued)

In most cases, pairing is accomplished by your Mac generating an 8-digit *passkey* that you must then type into the Bluetooth device (assuming that it has some kind of keypad). In other cases, the device comes with a default passkey that you must enter into your Mac to set up the pairing.

Connect a Bluetooth Device (continued)

CONNECT A BLUETOOTH KEYBOARD

1 Turn the keyboard on, if required.

2 Turn on the switch that makes the keyboard discoverable, if required.

3 Follow Steps **1** to **7** from earlier in this section.

Note: *In the Select Device Type dialog box, click the **Keyboard** option (○ changes to ⦿).*

The Bluetooth Keyboard Set Up dialog box appears.

4 Use the Bluetooth keyboard to type the displayed passkey.

CONNECT A BLUETOOTH HEADSET

1 Turn on the headset.

2 Turn on the switch that makes the headset discoverable.

3 Follow Steps **1** to **7** from earlier in this section.

Note: *In the Select Device Type dialog box, click the **Headset** option (○ changes to ⦿).*

The Bluetooth Headset Set Up dialog box appears.

4 Use the **Passkey** text box to type the headset's passkey.

CONNECT A BLUETOOTH CELL PHONE

1 Turn on the cell phone.

2 Make the cell phone discoverable.

3 Follow Steps **1** to **7** from earlier in this section.

Note: *In the Select Device Type dialog box, click the* **Mobile phone** *option (◯ changes to ◉).*

The Bluetooth Mobile Phone Set Up dialog box appears.

4 Use the Bluetooth phone's keypad to type the displayed passkey.

The Bluetooth Setup Assistant displays a list of services that your cell phone supports.

5 Deactivate the check box for any service you do not want to use (☑ changes to ☐).

6 Click **Continue.**

TIP

How do I remove a Bluetooth device?
Follow these steps:

1 Click 🚺 in the menu bar.

2 Click **Open Bluetooth Preferences.**

You can also click 🖥, click **System Preferences,** and then click **Bluetooth.**

The Bluetooth preferences appear.

3 Click the device you want to remove.

4 Click Remove (–).

Your Mac asks you to confirm.

5 Click **Remove.**

Your Mac removes the device.

Connect Your Mac to Another Mac

You can share data such as documents, bookmarks, and downloads between two Macs by connecting those Macs using a network cable or a FireWire cable.

This task assumes that you do not have a local area network set up, so you need to connect the two Macs directly. In either case, you must enable file sharing to share data between the Macs.

Connect Your Mac to Another Mac

CONNECT USING A NETWORK CABLE

1. Attach one of the network cable's connectors to the network port on one of the Macs.

2. Attach the other network cable connector to the network port on the other Mac.

CONNECT USING A FIREWIRE CABLE

1. Attach one of the FireWire cable's connectors to the FireWire port on one of the Macs.

2. Attach the other FireWire cable connector to the FireWire port on the other Mac.

ENABLE FILE SHARING

1 Click .

2 Click **System Preferences.**

The System Preferences window appears.

3 Click **Sharing.**

TIP

Can I use a regular network cable?
Yes, for many Macs. However, some older Macs require a special crossover cable. You must use such a cable if you want to connect any of the Macs in the following list:

eMac
iBook
iBook (FireWire)
iMac
iMac (17-inch Flat Panel)
iMac (Early 2001)

iMac (Flat Panel)
iMac (Slot Loading)
iMac (Summer 2000)
iMac (Summer 2001)
Power Mac G4 (AGP Graphics)
Power Mac G4 (PCI Graphics)

Power Mac G4 Cube
Power Macintosh G3 (Blue and White)
PowerBook (FireWire)
PowerBook G3 Series (Bronze Keyboard)

You must enable file sharing on both Macs. Once you have done that, you can see the files shared on the other Mac by accessing Finder's Network folder.

The Sharing preferences appear.

④ Click **File Sharing** (changes to ☑).

Note: *See the Tip on the following page to learn how to share other folders on your Mac.*

⑤ Click .

VIEW THE OTHER MAC'S FILES

① Click .

② Click the icon for the other Mac.

Note: *If you do not see an icon for the other Mac, click* **Go** *and then click* **Network***, or press* Shift + ⌘ +K.

- Your Mac connects to the other Mac using the Guest account.

3 Click **Connect As.**

Your Mac prompts you to log in to the other Mac.

4 Use the **Name** text box to type the user name of an account on the other Mac.

5 Use the **Password** text box to type the password of an account on the other Mac.

6 Click **Connect.**

Your Mac logs in to the other Mac.

- You see the folder associated with the user account that you used to log in to the other Mac.

7 Click a folder to see and work with its contents.

 TIP

How do I share other folders?

By default, your Mac shares just your user account's Public folder. Follow these steps to share another folder:

1 Click [icon].

2 Click **System Preferences.**

The System Preferences window appears.

3 Click **Sharing.**

4 Under the Shared Folders list, click [+].

5 Click the folder you want to share.

6 Click **Add.**

CHAPTER

4

Learning Mac Basics

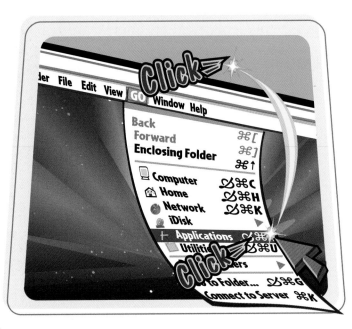

The OS X operating system is installed on all new Macintosh computers. You can use OS X to start programs, manage files, connect to the Internet, and perform computer maintenance, and so it is important to have a basic understanding of how OS X works.

Before you can begin to understand how the OS X operating system works, you should become familiar with the basic screen elements.

Menu Bar

The menu bar contains the pull-down menus for OS X and most OS X software.

Desktop

This is the OS X work area. It is where you work with your programs and documents.

Mouse Pointer

When you move your mouse, the pointer moves along with it.

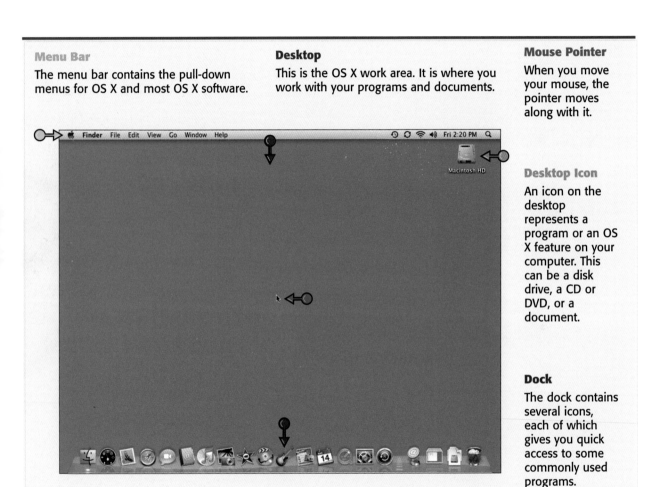

Desktop Icon

An icon on the desktop represents a program or an OS X feature on your computer. This can be a disk drive, a CD or DVD, or a document.

Dock

The dock contains several icons, each of which gives you quick access to some commonly used programs.

The Dock gives you one-click access to programs, folders, and documents.

Finder

You use Finder to work with the files on your computer.

Dashboard

You use Dashboard to access several cool and handy mini applications called *widgets*.

Mail

You use Mail to send and receive e-mail messages.

Safari

You use Safari to browse the World Wide Web on the Internet.

iChat

You use iChat to converse with other people in real time by sending each other text messages.

Address Book

You use the Address Book to store people's names, addresses, phone numbers, and other contact information.

iTunes

You use iTunes to play music files and audio CDs and to add music to your iPod.

iPhoto

You use iPhoto to import and edit digital photos and other images.

iMovie

You use iMovie to import and edit digital video movies.

iDVD

You use iDVD to burn images or video to a DVD disc.

GarageBand

You use GarageBand to create songs, podcasts, and other audio files.

iWeb

You use iWeb to create Web pages.

iCal

You use iCal to record upcoming appointments, birthdays, meetings, and other events.

QuickTime Player

You use QuickTime Player to play audio and video files, music CDs, and other media.

System Preferences

You use System Preferences to customize your Mac.

Time Machine

You use Time Machine to access backups of your files.

Apple Mac OS X

The Apple Mac OS X icon takes you to the World Wide Web page for OS X.

Documents

You use Documents to display the contents of your Documents folder.

Downloads

You use Downloads to display the contents of your Downloads folder.

Trash

You use the Trash to delete files.

Start a Program

To work with any program, you must first tell OS X which program you want to run. OS X then launches the program and displays it on the desktop.

1 Click the **Finder** icon ().

If the program that you want to start has an icon in the Dock, you can click the icon to start the program and skip the rest of these steps.

The Finder window appears.

2 Click **Applications.**

Note: You can also navigate to Applications in any Finder window by pressing Shift + ⌘ + A.

The Applications window appears.

③ Double-click the icon of the program that you want to start.

If you see a folder icon (), it means that the program resides in its own folder, a storage area on the computer. Double-click to open the folder and then double-click the program icon.

● The program appears on the desktop.

● OS X adds a button for the program to the Dock and displays a blue smudge beneath the program icon to remind you that the program is running.

● The menu bar displays the menus associated with the program.

TIPS

How do I add an icon to the Dock for a program I use frequently?

First, start the program as described in Steps **1** to **3**. Ctrl+click or right-click the program's Dock icon and then click **Keep In Dock.**

How do I shut down a running program?

The easiest way is to Ctrl+click or right-click the program's Dock icon and then click **Quit.** Alternatively, you can press ⌘+Q.

Switch Between Programs

With OS X, if you are *multitasking* — running two or more programs at once — you can easily switch from one program to another.

① Click the Dock icon of the program to which you want to switch.

● OS X brings the program's windows to the foreground.

● The menu bar displays the menus associated with the program.

Note: *To switch between windows from the keyboard, press and hold* ⌘ *and repeatedly press until the window that you want is highlighted in the list of running programs. Release* ⌘ *to switch to the window.*

You work with a program by accessing the various features in the program window.

Close Button

Click the **Close** button (⊙) to remove the program window from the desktop, usually without exiting the program.

Minimize Button

Click the **Minimize** button (⊙) to remove the window from the desktop and display an icon for the currently open document in the right side of the Dock. The window is still open, but not active.

Maximize Button

Click the **Maximize** button (⊙) to enlarge the window so it can display all of its content.

Title Bar

The title bar displays the name of the program. In some programs, the title bar also displays the name of the open document. To move the window, click and drag the title bar.

Toolbar

The toolbar contains buttons that offer easy access to common program commands and features.

Show/Hide Toolbar

Click ⊡ to toggle the toolbar on and off.

Resize Button

Click and drag ⧄ in the lower-right corner of the window to make the window larger or smaller.

Horizontal Scroll Bar

Use the horizontal scroll bar to navigate left and right in a document. Click **Scroll Left** (◀) to navigate left, and click **Scroll Right** (▶) to navigate right.

Vertical Scroll Bar

Use the vertical scroll bar to navigate up and down in a document. Click **Scroll Up** (▲) to navigate up; click **Scroll Down** (▼) to navigate down.

Status Bar

The status bar displays information about the current state of the program or document.

Select a Command from a Pull-Down Menu

When you are working in a program, you can use the menu bar to access the program's commands and features.

The items in a menu are either commands that execute an action in the program, or features that you can turn on and off.

Select a Command from a Pull-Down Menu

EXECUTE COMMANDS

1 Click the name of the menu that you want to display.

● The program displays the menu.

2 Click the command that you want to execute.

The program executes the command.

If your command appears in a submenu, first click the command that opens the submenu and then click the command that you want to run.

TURN FEATURES ON AND OFF

1 Click the name of the menu that you want to display.

● The program displays the menu.

2 Click the menu item.

You may have to click for a submenu if your command is not on the main menu.

The program turns the feature either on with a check mark (☑) or off (no check mark appears).

Select a Command Using a Toolbar

You can access commands faster using the toolbar. Most programs come with a toolbar, which is a collection of buttons that gives you one-click access to the program's most-common features.

Select a Command Using a Toolbar

TURN FEATURES ON AND OFF

1 Click the toolbar button that represents the feature you want to turn on.

● The program turns the feature on and indicates this state by highlighting the toolbar button.

● When a feature is turned off, the program does not highlight the button.

EXECUTE COMMANDS

1 Click the toolbar button that represents the command that you want.

2 If the button displays a menu, click the command on the menu.

● The program executes the command.

Dialog boxes appear when a program needs you to provide information. For example, when you select the File menu's Print command to print a document, you use the Print dialog box to specify the number of copies that you want to print. You provide that and other information by accessing various types of dialog box controls.

Command Button

Clicking a command button executes the command written on the button face. For example, you can click **OK** to apply settings that you have chosen in a dialog box, or you can click **Cancel** to close the dialog box without changing the settings.

Text Box

A text box enables you to enter typed text. Use the Del key to delete any existing characters, and then type your text.

List Box

A list box displays a list of choices from which you select the item you want. Use the vertical scroll bar to bring the item you want into view, and then click the item to select it.

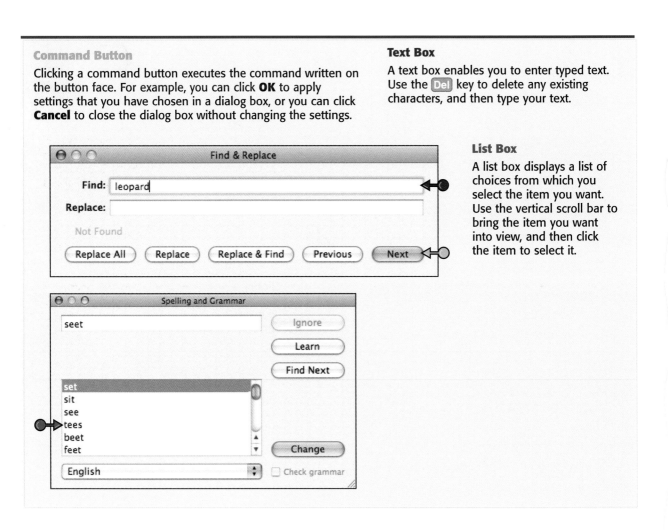

Pop-Up Menu

A pop-up menu displays a list of choices from which you select the item you want. Click ⟐ to pop up the menu, and then click the item that you want to select.

Check Box

Clicking a check box toggles a program feature on and off. If you are turning on a feature, the check box changes from ☐ to ☑; if you are turning off the feature, the check box changes from ☑ to ☐.

Radio Button

Clicking a radio button turns on a program feature. Only one radio button in a group can be turned on at a time. When you click a radio button, it changes from ○ to ◉.

Save a Document

After you create a document and make changes to it, you can save the document to preserve your work.

When you work on a document, OS X stores the changes in your computer's memory, which is erased each time you shut down your computer. Saving the document preserves your changes on your computer's hard drive.

① Click **File.**

② Click **Save.**

In most programs, you can also press ⌘+S.

If you have saved the document previously, your changes are now preserved, and you do not need to follow the rest of the steps in this section.

● If this is a new document that you have never saved before, the Save dialog appears.

③ Click in the **Save As** text box and type the name that you want to use for the document.

● To select a different folder in which to store the file, you can click ⬍ in the Where list and then click the location that you prefer.

④ Click **Save.**

The program saves the file.

Open a
Document

To work with a document that
you have saved in the past, you
can open it in the program that
you used to create it.

Open a Document

① Start the program that you want to
work with.

② Click **File.**

③ Click **Open.**

In most programs, you can also
press ⌘+O.

● The Open dialog appears.

● To select a different folder from
which to open the file, you can click
in the From list and then click the
location that you prefer.

④ Click the document.

⑤ Click **Open.**

The document appears in the
program window.

Print a
Document

When you need a hard copy of
your document, either for your
files or to distribute to someone
else, you can send the document
to your printer.

① Turn on your printer.

② Open the document that you
want to print.

③ Click **File.**

④ Click **Print.**

In many programs, you can select
the Print command by pressing
⌘+P.

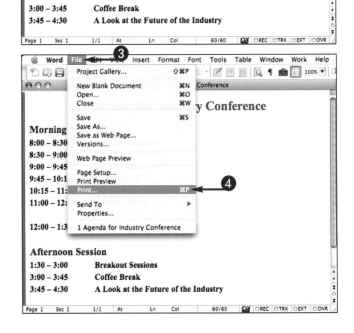

The Print dialog box appears.

The layout of the Print dialog box varies from program to program. The version shown here is a typical example.

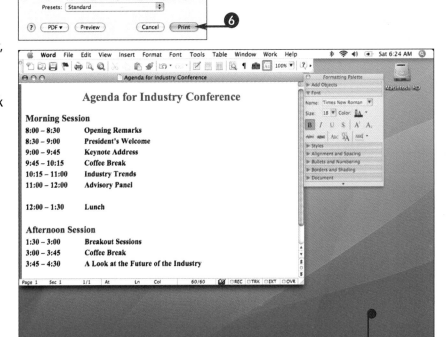

⑤ If you have more than one printer, click ⬦ in the Printer list to select the printer that you want to use.

● To print more than one copy, click to expand the dialog box, and then use the Copies text box to type the number of copies to print.

⑥ Click **Print.**

Agenda for Industry Conference

Morning Session

8:00 – 8:30	Opening Remarks
8:30 – 9:00	President's Welcome
9:00 – 9:45	Keynote Address
9:45 – 10:15	Coffee Break
10:15 – 11:00	Industry Trends
11:00 – 12:00	Advisory Panel
12:00 – 1:30	Lunch

Afternoon Session

1:30 – 3:00	Breakout Sessions
3:00 – 3:45	Coffee Break
3:45 – 4:30	A Look at the Future of the Industry

● OS X prints the document. The print icon appears in the Dock while the document prints.

TIP

Can I preview my document before I print it?

Yes. It is a good idea to preview the document before printing it to ensure that the document layout looks the way you want. To preview the document, follow Steps **1** to **4** in this section to display the Print dialog box. Click **Preview** to display the document in the Preview window. When you are done, click **Preview** and then click **Quit Preview.**

Edit Document Text

When you work with a character-based file, such as a text or word-processing document or an e-mail message, you need to know the basic techniques for editing, selecting, copying, and moving text.

Edit Document Text

DELETE CHARACTERS

① In a text document, click immediately to the right of the last character that you want to delete.

● The cursor appears after the character.

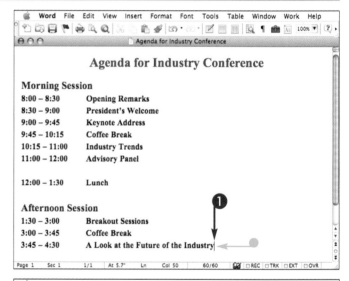

② Press Del until you have deleted all the characters you want.

If you make a mistake, immediately click **Edit,** and then click **Undo.** You can also press ⌘+Z.

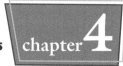

SELECT TEXT FOR EDITING

① Click and drag across the text that you want to select.

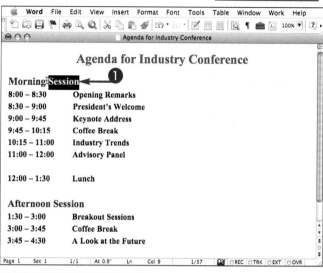

② Release the mouse button.

● The program highlights the selected text.

Are there any shortcut methods for selecting text?
Yes, most OS X programs have shortcuts you can use. Here are the most useful ones:

● Double-click a word to select it.

● Triple-click inside a paragraph to select it. (In Word, triple-click to select a line, quadruple-click to select a paragraph.)

● Press ⌘+A to select the entire document.

continued

Once you select text, you can then copy or move the text to another location in your document.

COPY TEXT

1 Select the text that you want to copy.

2 Click **Edit.**

3 Click **Copy.**

In most programs, you can also press ⌘+C.

4 Click inside the document at the position where you want the copy of the text to appear.

The cursor appears in the position where you clicked.

5 Click **Edit.**

6 Click **Paste.**

In most programs, you can also press ⌘+V.

● The program inserts a copy of the selected text at the cursor position.

MOVE TEXT

① Select the text that you want to move.

② Click **Edit.**

③ Click **Cut.**

In most programs, you can also press ⌘+X.

The program removes the text from the document.

④ Click inside the document at the position where you want to move the text.

The cursor appears at the position where you clicked.

⑤ Click **Edit.**

⑥ Click **Paste.**

In most programs, you can also press ⌘+V.

● The program inserts the text at the cursor position.

How do I move and copy text with my mouse?

First, select the text that you want to move or copy. To move the selected text, position the mouse pointer over the selection and then click and drag the text to the new position within the document.

To copy the selected text, position the mouse pointer over the selection, press and hold the Option key, and then click and drag the text to the new position within the document.

Copy a File

You can make an exact copy of a file. This is useful when you want to make a backup of an important file or if you want to send the copy on a disk to another person.

You can copy either a single file or multiple files. You can also use this technique to copy a folder.

Copy a File

1 Locate the file that you want to copy.

2 Open the folder to which you want to copy the file.

To open a second folder window, click **File** and then click **New Finder Window,** or press ⌘+N.

3 Press and hold the **Option** key, and then click and drag the file and drop it inside the destination folder.

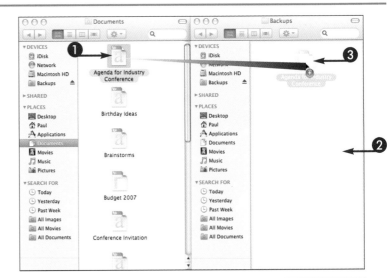

● The original file remains in its folder.

● A copy of the original file appears in the destination folder.

You can also make a copy of a file in the same folder, which is useful if you want to make major changes to the file and you would like to preserve a copy of the original. Click the file, click **File,** and then click **Duplicate,** or press ⌘+D. OS X creates a copy with the word "copy" added to the filename.

Move a File

When you need to store a file in a new location, the easiest way is to move the file from its current folder to another folder on your computer.

You can use this technique to move a single file, multiple files, and even a folder.

Move a File

① Locate the file that you want to move.

② Open the folder to which you want to move the file.

To create a new destination folder in the current folder, click **File** and then click **New Folder,** or press Shift + ⌘ + N.

③ Click and drag the file and drop it inside the destination folder.

● The file disappears from its original folder.

● The file moves to the destination folder.

Rename a File

You can change the name of a file, which is useful if the current filename does not accurately describe the contents of the file. By giving your document a descriptive name, you make it easier to find the file later.

You should only rename those documents that you have created or that have been given to you by someone else. Do not rename any of the OS X system files or any files associated with your programs, or your computer may behave erratically, or even crash.

Rename a File

① Open the folder containing the file that you want to rename.

② Click the file.

③ Press **Return**.

● A text box appears around the filename.

You can also rename any folders that you have created.

④ Edit the existing name or type a new name that you want to use for the file.

If you decide that you do not want to rename the file after all, you can press **Esc** to cancel the operation.

⑤ Press **Return** or click an empty section of the folder.

● The new name appears under the file icon.

Delete a File

When you no longer need a file, you can delete it. This helps to prevent your hard drive from becoming cluttered with unnecessary files.

You should ensure that you delete only those documents that you have created or that have been given to you by someone else. Do not delete any of the OS X system files or any files associated with your programs, or your computer may behave erratically, or even crash.

Delete a File

① Locate the file that you want to delete.

② Click and drag the file and drop it on the Trash icon in the Dock.

● The file disappears from the folder.

If you delete a file accidentally, you can restore it. Simply click the Dock's Trash icon to open the Trash window. Click and drag the file from the Trash window and drop it back in its original folder.

Playing and Organizing Music

Using iTunes, you can create a library of music and use that library to play songs, albums, and collections of songs called playlists, tune in to an Internet radio station, and subscribe to podcasts. You can also use iTunes to listen to music CDs, manage music on an iPod, and purchase music from the online iTunes Store.

Open and Close iTunes

Your Mac includes iTunes to enable you to play back and manage various types of audio files. To begin using the program, you must first learn how to find and open the iTunes window. When you finish using the program, you can close the iTunes window to free up computer processing power.

Open and Close iTunes

OPEN ITUNES

① Click **Finder** (🔲) in the Dock.

② Click **Applications**.

③ Double-click **iTunes**.

The iTunes window appears.

CLOSE ITUNES

1 Click **iTunes.**

2 Click **Quit iTunes.**

 TIPS

Are there faster methods I can use to open iTunes?

The fastest way to start iTunes is to click the iTunes icon ( ) in the Dock. If you have used iTunes recently, another reasonably fast method is to click the Apple icon ( ), click **Recent Items,** and then click **iTunes.**

Are there faster methods I can use to close iTunes?

Probably the fastest method you can use to quit iTunes is to click **Close** ( ). Alternatively, Ctrl+click or right-click and then click **Quit.** Finally, if your hands are closer to the keyboard than to the mouse, you can quit iTunes by pressing ⌘+Q.

Understanding the iTunes Library

Most of your iTunes time will be spent in the Library, so you need to understand what you are working with.

The iTunes Library

The iTunes Library is where your Mac stores the files that you can play and work with in the iTunes application. The iTunes Library includes not only the audio features discussed in this chapter, but also movies, TV shows, and games. Each section of the Library shows you the contents of that section and the details for each item, such as the name of each song and the artist who recorded it.

Audio in the Library

Although iTunes has some video components, its focus is on audio features, so most of the Library sections are audio related. These sections include Music, Podcasts, Audiobooks, and Radio. If you connect an iPhone to your Mac, your iTunes Library also includes a Ringtones section for music-based ringtones.

Familiarizing yourself with the various elements of the iTunes window is a good idea so that you can easily navigate and activate elements when you are ready to play audio files, podcasts, or listen to Internet radio.

Playback Controls

These buttons control media playback, and enable you to make adjustments to the volume.

Status Area

This area displays information about the item that is currently playing or the action that iTunes is currently performing.

View Options

You use these buttons to control how the contents of the current category appear.

Contents

The contents of the current iTunes Library category appear here.

Categories

This area displays the iTunes Library categories that you can view.

Now Playing

This area shows a visual display of the currently playing item, usually the album art.

You use the Music category of the iTunes Library to play a song that is stored on your computer. If you need to leave the room or take a call, you can also pause the currently playing song.

Play a Song

① Click **Music.**

② Click the song you want to play.

③ Click the **Play** button (▶).

iTunes begins playing the song.

● Information about the song playback appears here.

● iTunes displays a speaker icon (🔊) beside the currently playing song.

● If you need to stop the song temporarily, click the **Pause** button (⏸).

Note: *You can also pause and restart a song by pressing the* Spacebar.

Note: *See the "Play a Music CD" section to learn more about the playback buttons.*

You can adjust the volume in iTunes up or down to get the audio just right. You can also mute the playback to turn off the volume.

Adjust the Volume

TURN VOLUME UP OR DOWN

1 Click and drag the **Volume** slider left (to reduce the volume) or right (to increase the volume).

Note: To reduce the volume, you can also press ⌘+⬇; to increase the volume, you can also press ⌘+⬆.

MUTE THE VOLUME

1 Click **Controls.**

2 Click **Mute.**

Note: To mute the volume, you can also press **Option** + ⌘ + ⬇.

Note: To restore the volume, either click **Control** and then **Mute**, or adjust the Volume slider.

Play a Music CD

You can play your favorite music CDs in iTunes. The CD appears in the Devices section and it displays the individual tracks on the CD. During playback, you can skip tracks and pause and resume play.

Play a Music CD

PLAY A CD

① Insert a music CD into your Mac's CD or DVD drive.

● The music CD appears in iTune's Devices category.

● iTunes shows the contents of the CD.

② Click .

iTunes begins playing the CD from the first track.

SKIP A TRACK

③ Click the **Next** button (⏭) to skip to the next track.

Note: *You can also skip to the next track by pressing ⌘+→.*

④ Click the **Previous** button (⏮) to skip to the beginning of the current track; click ⏮ again to skip to the previous track.

Note: *You can also skip to the previous track by pressing ⌘+←.*

PAUSE AND RESUME PLAY

⑤ Click ⏸ (⏸ changes to ▶).

iTunes pauses playback.

⑥ Click ▶.

iTunes resumes playback where you left off.

TIPS

Can I change the CD's audio levels?

Yes, iTunes has a graphic equalizer component that you can use to adjust the levels. To display the equalizer, click **View** and then click **Show Equalizer**. In the Equalizer window, use the sliders to set the audio levels, or click the **drop-down list** (▯) to choose an audio preset.

Can I display visualizations during playback?

Yes. You can click **View** and then click **Turn On Visualizer** (you can also press ⌘+T). To change the currently displayed visualizer, click **View,** click **Visualizer,** and then click the visualization you want to view.

continued

iTunes gives you more options for controlling the CD playback. For example, you can switch to another song, set the CD to repeat, and play the tracks randomly. When the CD is done, you can use iTunes to eject it from your Mac.

Play a Music CD *(continued)*

PLAY ANOTHER SONG

⑦ In the list of songs, double-click the song you want to play.

   iTunes begins playing the song.

REPEAT THE CD

⑧ Click the **Repeat** button (changes to).

   iTunes restarts the CD after the last track finishes playing.

   To repeat just the current song, click again (changes to).

PLAY SONGS RANDOMLY

9 Click the **Shuffle** button
(⤨ changes to ⤨).

iTunes shuffles the order of play.

EJECT THE CD

10 Click the **Eject** button (⏏)
beside the CD.

● You can also click the **Eject**
button (⏏) in the lower-right
corner of the iTunes window.

*Note: You can also eject the CD by pressing and
holding the Eject key on the keyboard.*

iTunes ejects the CD from your
Mac's CD or DVD drive.

Why do I not see the song titles after I insert my music CD?

When you play a music CD, iTunes tries to gather information about the album
from the CD itself. If that does not work, iTunes tries to get the album data from
the Internet. If you still see only track numbers, it may be that you do not have
an Internet connection established. Connect to the Internet, click **Advanced,** and
then click **Get CD Track Names.**

Import Tracks from a Music CD

You can add tracks from a music CD to the iTunes Library. This enables you to listen to an album without having to put the CD into your Mac's CD or DVD drive each time. The process of adding tracks from a CD is called *importing*, or *ripping*, in Mac OS X.

After you import the tracks from a music CD, you can play those tracks from the Music category of the iTunes Library.

Import Tracks from a Music CD

① Insert a CD into your Mac's CD or DVD drive.

● The music CD appears in iTune's Devices category.

● iTunes shows the contents of the CD.

② Click the check box so it is unchecked next to each CD track that you do not want to copy (☐ changes to ☑).

③ Click **Import CD**.

iTunes begins importing the track or tracks.

● This area displays the copy progress for each track.

● When iTunes is importing a track, it displays ⬚ beside the track number.

● When iTunes is finished importing a track, it displays ⊘ beside the track number.

● When iTunes has completed the import, you see ⊘ beside the track numbers of all the tracks you selected.

 TIPS

I ripped a track by accident. How do I remove it from the Library?

Click the **Music** category, scroll down until you see the album you imported, Ctrl+click or right-click the track that you want to remove, and then click **Delete** from the pop-up menu. When iTunes asks you to confirm the deletion, click **Remove**. When iTunes asks if you want to keep the file, click **Move to Trash**.

Can I adjust the quality of the copies?

Yes. You do that by changing the *bit rate*, which is a measure of how much of the CD's original data gets copied to your computer. This is measured in kilobits per second (Kbps): the higher the value the higher the quality, but the more disk space each track takes up. Click **iTunes,** click **Preferences,** click **Advanced,** and then click **Importing.** In the **Setting** list, click ⬚, click **Custom,** and then use the Stereo Bit Rate list to click the value you want.

Create a Playlist

A *playlist* is a collection of songs that are related in some way. Using your iTunes Library, you can create customized playlists that include only the songs that you want to hear.

Create a Playlist

CREATE THE PLAYLIST

1 Click **File**.

2 Click **New Playlist**.

Note: You can also choose the New Playlist command by pressing ⌘ + N.

iTunes creates a new playlist.

3 Type a name for the new playlist.

4 Press Return.

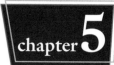

ADD SONGS TO THE PLAYLIST

1 Click **Music.**

2 Ctrl +click or right-click a song that you want to add to the new playlist.

3 Click **Add to Playlist.**

4 Click the playlist you just created.

5 Repeat Steps **2** to **4** to add more songs to the playlist.

6 Click the playlist.

● iTunes displays the songs you added to the playlist.

● If you want to listen to the playlist, you can click ►.

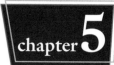
TIPS

Is there a faster way to create and populate a playlist?

Yes. First, click **Music** to open the Music category of the iTunes Library. Press and hold the ⌘ key and then click each song that you want to include in your playlist. When you are done, click **File** and then click **New Playlist from Selection**. (You can also press Option + ⌘ + N.) Type the new playlist name and then press Return.

Is there any way to make iTunes add songs to a playlist automatically?

Yes, you can create a *smart playlist* where the songs that appear in the list have one or more properties in common, such as the genre, rating, artist, or text in the song title. Click **File** and then click **New Smart Playlist** (you can also press Option + ⌘ + N). Use the Smart Playlist dialog box to create one or more rules that define which songs you want to appear in the playlist.

Burn Music Files to a CD

You can copy, or *burn*, music files from your Mac onto a CD. Burning CDs is a great way to create customized CDs that you can listen to on the computer or in a portable device. You can burn music files from within the iTunes window.

To burn music files to a CD, your Mac must have a recordable CD or DVD drive.

Burn Music Files to a CD

1 Insert a blank CD into your Mac's recordable disc drive.

2 If you already have iTunes running and your Mac asks you to choose an action, click **Ignore.**

● If you do not yet have iTunes running, use the Action menu to click [icon], click **Open iTunes,** and then click **OK.**

3 Create a playlist for the songs you want to burn to the disc.

Note: *See the section "Create a Playlist" to learn how to build an iTunes playlist.*

4 Click the playlist that you want to burn.

5 Click the heading of the play order column to ensure the songs are sorted in the order they will play on the disc.

6 To modify the play order, click and drag a song and drop it on a new position in the playlist.

7 Repeat Step **6** to get the songs in the order that you want them to appear on the CD.

● To arrange the songs randomly, click **iTunes Shuffle** (⤨).

8 Click **File.**

9 Click **Burn Playlist to Disc.**

● You can also click the **Burn Disc** button.

iTunes burns the songs to the CD.

Can I control the interval between songs on the CD?

Yes. By default, iTunes adds 2 seconds between each track on the CD. To change that, click **iTunes,** click **Preferences,** click **Advanced,** and then click **Burning.** In the Gap Between Songs pop-up menu, click ⬍, and then click the interval you want to use. Click **OK.**

What happens if I have more music than can fit on a single disc?

You can still add all the music you want to burn to the playlist. iTunes fills the first disc and then adds the remaining songs to a second disc. After iTunes finishes burning the first disc, it prompts you to insert the next one.

Edit Song Information

For each song in your Library or a music CD, iTunes maintains a collection of information that includes the song title, artist, album title, genre, and more. If there are errors or omissions in a song's information, you can edit the data.

You can edit one song at a time, or you can edit multiple songs, such as an entire music CD.

Edit Song Information

EDIT A SINGLE SONG

1 Click the song you want to edit.

2 Click **File.**

3 Click **Get Info.**

Note: You can also press ⌘+I. *Alternatively,* Ctrl *+click or right-click the song and then click* Get Info.

4 Click **Info.**

5 Edit or add information to the fields.

● If you want to edit a nearby song, click **Previous** or **Next** to display the song you want.

6 Click **OK.**

EDIT MULTIPLE SONGS

1 Select all the songs that you want to edit.

Note: To select individual songs, press and hold ⌘ and click each song; to select all songs (on a music CD, for example), press ⌘+A.

2 Click **File**.

3 Click **Get Info**.

Note: You can also press ⌘+I. Alternatively, Ctrl+click or right-click any selected song and then click Get Info.

iTunes asks you to confirm that you want to edit multiple songs.

4 Click **Yes**.

The Multiple Item Information dialog box appears.

5 Edit or add information to the fields.

● iTunes displays ☑ beside each modified field.

6 Click **OK**.

iTunes applies the edits to each selected song.

TIP

When I edit multiple songs, why do I not see all the fields in the Multiple Item Information dialog box?

When you are editing multiple songs, you can only modify fields that contain data that is common to all the songs. This makes sense because any changes you make apply to all the selected songs. For example, each song has a different title, so you would not want to give every song the same title. This is why you do not see the Name field in the Multiple Item Information dialog box. However, you do see fields that are common to all the selected songs. On a music CD, for example, data such as the artist, album title, and genre are usually the same for all the songs.

Purchase Music from the iTunes Store

You can add music to your iTunes Library by purchasing it from the iTunes Store. iTunes downloads the song or album to your computer and then adds it to both the Music section and the Purchased section.

To purchase music from the iTunes Store, you must have an Apple account. This can either be an account on the Apple Store site or a MobileMe account. You can also use an AOL account, if you have one.

Purchase Music from the iTunes Store

① Click **iTunes Store.**

② Click **Music.**

The iTunes Store appears.

③ Locate the music you want to purchase.

④ Click **Buy Album.**

● If you just want to purchase a song, click **Buy Song** instead.

iTunes asks you to confirm the purchase.

5 Click **Buy.**

iTunes charges your credit card and begins downloading the music to your Mac.

● To watch the progress of the download, click **Downloads.**

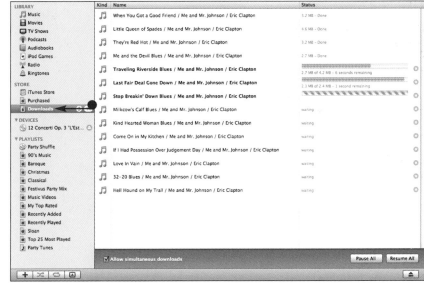

When the download is complete, iTunes asks if you want to back up your purchased music.

6 Click **Not Now.**

● If you prefer to back up your purchase now, click **Back Up Purchases** and then follow the instructions that appear.

Can I use my purchased music on other computers and devices?

Yes, with some restrictions. You can play most songs on up to five computers, on your iPod, through Apple TV, or burned to an audio CD. These restrictions are part of the digital rights management (DRM) applied to most songs. The iTunes Plus sections of the store offer some DRM-free songs that usually cost more, but do not have these restrictions.

If I want to purchase a number of songs, how do I avoid having many $0.99 charges on my credit card bill?

You can switch your iTunes Store preferences to use a shopping cart instead of the default 1-Click purchasing. Click **iTunes,** click **Preferences,** click **Store,** click **Buy using a Shopping Cart** (○ changes to ◉), and then click **OK.** When shopping, you now click **Add Album** (or **Add Song**) to add music to your shopping cart. When you are done, click **Shopping Cart** in iTunes, and then click **Buy Now.**

Listen to an Internet Radio Station

The Internet offers a number of radio stations that you can listen to. iTunes maintains a list of many of these online radio stations, so it is often easier to use iTunes to listen to Internet radio.

Just like a regular radio station, an Internet radio station broadcasts a constant audio stream, except you access the audio over the Internet instead of over the air.

Listen to an Internet Radio Station

① Click **Radio**.

iTunes displays a list of radio genres.

② Click ▶ to open the genre you want to work with (▶ changes to ▼).

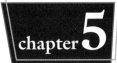

iTunes displays a list of radio station streams in the genre.

③ Click the radio station stream you want to listen to.

④ Click ▶.

iTunes plays the radio station stream.

● The name of the station and the name of the currently playing track usually appear here.

Is it possible to save or record a song from a radio station stream?

No, an Internet radio stream is "listen-only." iTunes does not give you any way to save the stream to your Mac hard disk or to record the stream as it plays.

In the Radio section of the iTunes Library, what does the Bit Rate column refer to?

The bit rate is measured in kilobits per second (Kbps) and is the rate at which the Internet radio station broadcasts the stream. The higher the rate, the better the music quality, but higher rates also require a fast Internet connection. Some stations offer multiple bit rates, so if a stream is choppy or distorted, try listening to a lower bit rate stream.

Subscribe to a Podcast

A *podcast* is an audio feed — or sometimes a feed that combines both audio and video — that a publisher updates regularly with new episodes. The easiest way to get each episode is to subscribe to the podcast. This ensures that iTunes automatically downloads each new episode to your iTunes Library.

You can subscribe to podcasts either directly via the publisher's Web site, or via the iTunes Store.

Subscribe to a Podcast

SUBSCRIBE TO A PODCAST ON THE WEB

1 Use your Web browser to navigate to the podcast's home page.

2 Click the **Subscribe in iTunes** link.

*Note: In some cases, the link is called **Add to iTunes** or simply **iTunes**.*

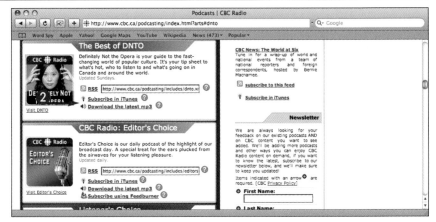

● iTunes begins downloading the available episodes.

● The podcast subscription appears in the Library's Podcasts category.

**SUBSCRIBE TO A PODCAST
USING THE ITUNES STORE**

1 Click **iTunes Store.**

2 Click **Podcasts.**

3 Locate the podcast you want to subscribe to.

4 Click **Subscribe.**

● If you just want to listen to one episode before subscribing, click **Get Episode** instead.

iTunes asks you to confirm.

5 Click **Subscribe.**

iTunes adds the subscription to the Podcasts category of the Library.

What do I do if the podcast Web site does not have an iTunes link?

In this case, you can subscribe to the podcast by telling iTunes the address of the podcast's feed. Follow these steps:

1 On the podcast Web site, copy the address of the podcast feed.

2 In iTunes, click **Advanced.**

3 Click **Subscribe to Podcast.**

The Subscribe to Podcast dialog appears.

4 Use the **URL** text box to paste (or type) the address of the podcast feed.

5 Click **OK.**

iTunes downloads the available episodes and adds the subscription to the Podcasts category of the Library.

Viewing and Editing Your Photos

Whether you just want to look at your photos, or you want to edit your photos to crop out unneeded portions or fix problems, your Mac comes with a number of useful tools for working with your photos.

View a Preview of a Photo

You can preview any saved image file using views such as Columns or Cover Flow in the Pictures folder. You can also preview photos using the Preview application.

To use Cover Flow to preview a photo, you must have Mac OS X 10.5 (Leopard) or later.

View a Preview of a Photo

VIEW A PREVIEW IN FINDER

1. Click **Finder** (🖼) in the Dock.

2. Click **Pictures.**

3. Click the folder that contains the photo you want to preview.

4. Click the photo.

5. Click **Columns.**

- Finder displays a preview of the photo.

VIEW A PREVIEW WITH COVER FLOW

1. Click 🖼 in the Dock.

2. Click **Pictures.**

3. Click the folder that contains the photo you want to preview.

4. Click the photo.

5. Click **Cover Flow.**

- Finder displays a preview of the photo.

- Use the scroll bar to scroll through the other photos in the folder.

VIEW A PREVIEW IN THE PREVIEW APPLICATION

1 Click 🖼 in the Dock.

2 Click **Pictures.**

3 Open the folder that contains the photo you want to preview.

4 Double-click the photo.

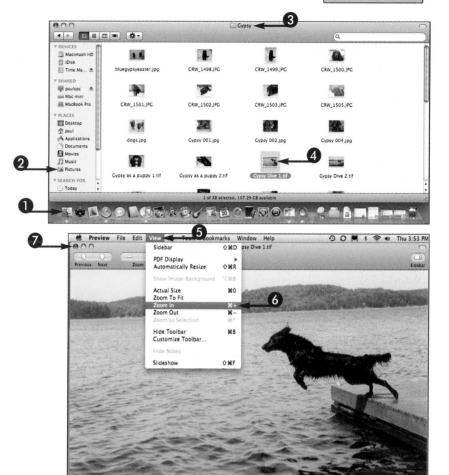

The Preview application opens and displays the photo.

5 Click **View.**

6 Use the View menu commands to change how the photo appears in the Preview window. For example, click **Zoom In** to get a closer look at the photo.

7 When you are finished viewing the photo, click **Close** (⬤).

TIPS

Is there an easier way to preview multiple photos using the Preview application?

Yes. Instead of constantly starting and quitting Preview for each photo you want to view, you can load multiple photos into the Preview application. In Finder, navigate to the folder that contains the photos, and then select each file that you want to preview. Either click and drag the mouse (▶) over the photos or press and hold ⌘ and click each one. In Preview, click **Next** and **Previous** to navigate the photos.

Is there a way that I can zoom in on just a portion of a photo?

Yes. Click **Tools** and then click **Select Tool** (or either press ⌘+3 or click **Select** in the toolbar). Click and drag your mouse ▶ to select the portion of the photo that you want to magnify. Click **View** and then click **Zoom to Selection** (or press ⌘+*).

View a Slideshow of Your Photos

You can easily view multiple photos by running them in a slideshow using the Preview application. The slideshow displays the images full-screen, and Preview automatically displays the next photo after a few seconds.

View a Slideshow of Your Photos

❶ Click 🖼 in the Dock.

❷ Click **Pictures.**

❸ Open the folder that contains the photos you want to view in the slideshow.

❹ Select the photos you want to view.

❺ Click **File.**

❻ Click **Open.**

The Preview application appears.

● The images you selected appear in the sidebar.

❼ To adjust the order of the photos, click and drag images in the sidebar.

❽ Click **Slideshow.**

Preview begins the slideshow.

9 Move the mouse ↖.

● Preview displays the slideshow controls.

● Click **Next** to move to the next photo.

● Click **Back** to move to the previous photo.

● Click **Pause** to suspend the slideshow.

10 When the slideshow is over or when you want to return to Preview, click **Close.**

Is it possible to jump to a specific photo during the slideshow?

Yes, by using the Index Sheet feature. In the slideshow controls, click the **Index Sheet** button. Preview displays thumbnail views of all the slideshow images. Click the photo that you want to view in the slideshow.

What keyboard shortcuts can I use when viewing a slideshow?

Press → to display the next photo, and press ← to display the previous photo. Press Spacebar to pause the slideshow, and press Spacebar to resume. Press Esc to end the slideshow. Press I to view the Index Sheet, use the arrow keys to select a photo, and then press Return to view it.

Open and Close iPhoto

Your Mac includes iPhoto to enable you to import photos from a digital camera, view photos, and edit and repair photos. To begin using the program, you must first learn how to find and open the iPhoto window. When you finish using the program, you can close the iPhoto window to free up computer-processing power.

OPEN IPHOTO

1. Click 🔲 in the Dock.
2. Click **Applications.**
3. Double-click **iPhoto.**

The iPhoto window appears.

CLOSE IPHOTO

1 Click **iPhoto.**

2 Click **Quit iPhoto.**

TIPS

Are there faster methods I can use to open iPhoto?

The fastest way to start iPhoto is to click the iPhoto icon (🌸) in the Dock. If you have used iPhoto recently, another reasonably fast method is to click 🍎, click **Recent Items,** and then click **iPhoto.**

Are there faster methods I can use to close iPhoto?

Probably the fastest method you can use to quit iPhoto is to click 🍎. Alternatively, Ctrl+click or right-click 🌸 and then click **Quit.** Finally, if your hands are closer to the keyboard than to the mouse, you can quit iPhoto by pressing ⌘+Q.

Import Photos from a Digital Camera

You can import photos from a digital camera and save them on your Mac. In most cases, your Mac uses the iPhoto application to handle importing photos.

See Chapter 3 to learn how to connect a digital camera to your Mac.

IMPORT PHOTOS FROM A DIGITAL CAMERA

1 Connect your digital camera to your Mac.

Your Mac launches the iPhoto application.

● Your digital camera appears in the iPhoto Devices section.

● iPhoto displays previews of the camera photos.

2 Use the Event Name text box to type a name for the group of photos you are going to import.

3 Use the Description text box to type a description of the photos you are going to import.

④ Select the photos that you want to import.

Note: To select photos, either click and drag the mouse (↖) around the photos you want, or press and hold ⌘ and click each photo.

⑤ Click **Import Selected.**

● If you want to import all the photos from the digital camera, click **Import All** instead.

iPhoto imports the photos from the digital camera.

iPhoto asks if you want to delete the original photos from the digital camera.

⑥ If you no longer need the photos on the camera, click **Delete Originals.**

● If you prefer to keep the photos on the camera, click **Keep Originals** instead.

VIEW THE IMPORTED PHOTOS

① Click **Events.**

② Double-click the event name that you specified in Step **2** on the previous page.

When I connect my digital camera, why do I see Image Capture instead of iPhoto?
You need to configure Image Capture to open iPhoto when you connect your camera. Follow these steps:

① Click 🖼 in the Dock and click **Applications.**

② Double-click **Image Capture.** The Image Capture application opens.

③ Click **Image Capture** in the menu bar and click **Preferences.**

④ In the **When a camera is connected, open** list, click 🔽, click **iPhoto,** then click **Close** (🔴).

View Your Photos

If you want to look at several photos, you can use iPhoto's full-screen mode to navigate backward and forward through the photos in a folder.

View Your Photos

❶ In iPhoto, click **Photos.**

❷ Click ▶ beside the folder that contains the photos you want to view (▶ changes to ▼).

❸ Click the first photo you want to view.

❹ Click **Enter full screen** (⬚).

iPhoto displays the photo in full-screen mode.

⑤ Move the mouse (↖) to the bottom of the screen.

iPhoto displays the full-screen controls.

⑥ Click **Next** (➡) to view the next photo in the folder.

● You can also click **Previous** (⬅) to see the previous photo in the folder.

Note: You can also navigate photos by pressing ➡ and ⬅.

⑦ When you are done, move the mouse ↖ to the bottom of the screen.

⑧ Click **Exit** (⊗).

TIP

Is there a way that I can jump quickly to a particular photo in full-screen mode?

Yes. Follow these steps:

① Move the mouse ↖ to the top of the screen.

● iPhoto displays thumbnail images of the folder's photos.

② Use the horizontal scroll bar to bring the thumbnail of the photo you want into view.

③ Click the photo's thumbnail.

iPhoto displays the photo in full-screen mode.

Create an Album

An *album* is a collection of photos that are related in some way. Using your iPhoto Library, you can create customized albums that include only the photos that you want to view.

Create an Album

CREATE AN ALBUM

① Click **File.**

② Click **New Album.**

Note: *You can also choose the New Album command by pressing* ⌘+N.

③ Type a name for the new album.

④ Click **Create.**

ADD PHOTOS TO THE ALBUM

① Click **Photos.**

② Click ▶ beside the folder that contains the photos you want to work with (▶ changes to ▼).

③ Click and drag a photo and drop it on the new album.

④ Repeat Steps **2** and **3** to add other photos to the album.

⑤ Click the album.

● iPhoto displays the photos you added to the album.

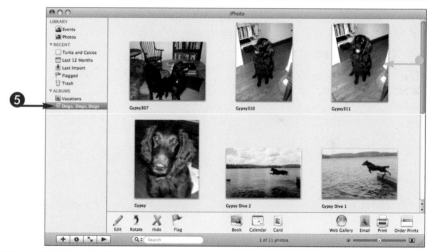

Is there a faster way to create and populate an album?

Yes. First, click **Photos** to open the Photos section of the iPhoto Library, and then open the folder you want to work with. Press and hold the ⌘ key and then click each photo that you want to include in your album. When you are done, click **File** and then click **New Album from Selection.** (You can also press Shift+⌘+N.) Type the new album name and then click **Create.**

Is there any way to make iPhoto add photos to an album automatically?

Yes, you can create a *smart album* where the photos that appear in the album have one or more properties in common, such as the description, rating, date, or text in the photo title. Click **File** and then click **New Smart Album** (you can also press Option+⌘+N). Use the Smart Album dialog box to create one or more rules that define which photos you want to appear in the album.

If you have a photo containing elements that you do not want or need to see, you can often cut out those elements. This is called *cropping*, and it can help give focus to the true subject of a photo.

When you crop a photo, you specify a rectangular area of the photo that you want to keep. iPhoto discards everything outside of the rectangle.

Crop a Photo

① Click the photo you want to crop.

② Click **Edit.**

iPhoto displays its editing tools.

③ Click **Crop (□).**

iPhoto displays a cropping rectangle on the photo.

④ Click and drag a corner or side to define the area you want to keep.

Note: Remember that iPhoto keeps the area inside the rectangle.

⑤ Click **Apply.**

iPhoto saves the cropped photo.

⑥ Click **Done.**

iPhoto exits Edit mode.

TIP

Is there a quick way to crop a photo to a certain size?

Yes, iPhoto enables you to specify either a specific size, such as 640 x 480, or a specific ratio, such as 4 x 3 or 16 x 9. Follow these steps:

① Follow Steps **1** to **3** to display the Crop tool.

② In the **Constrain** list, click ⬍.

③ Click the size or ratio you want to use.

④ Click **Apply.**

Rotate a Photo

If you have a photo that shows the subject sideways or upside down, you can use iPhoto to rotate the photo so that the subject appears right-side up. You can rotate a photo either clockwise or counterclockwise.

① Click the photo you want to rotate.

② Click **Edit**.

iPhoto displays its editing tools.

③ Click **Rotate** (↺).

● iPhoto rotates the photo 90 degrees counterclockwise.

④ Repeat Step **3** until the subject of the photo is right-side up.

⑤ Click **Done.**

iPhoto exits Edit mode.

TIP

Can I rotate a photo clockwise, instead?
Yes, you can. Press and hold the Option key and the Rotate icon changes from ↥ to ↧. With Option held down, click **Rotate** to rotate the photo clockwise by 90 degrees. Note, too, that you can also Ctrl+click or right-click the photo and then click **Rotate Clockwise.**

Straighten a Photo

If you have a photo that is not quite level, you can use iPhoto to nudge the photo clockwise or counterclockwise so that the subject appears straight.

① Click the photo you want to straighten.

② Click **Edit.**

iPhoto displays its editing tools.

③ Click **Straighten** (📷).

iPhoto displays a grid over the photo.

④ Click **Decrease Angle** (▣) to nudge the photo 0.1 degrees counterclockwise.

● You can also click **Increase Angle** (▣) to nudge the photo 0.1 degrees clockwise.

⑤ Click **Done.**

iPhoto exits Edit mode.

How do I know when my photo is level?

Use the gridlines that iPhoto places over the photo. Locate a horizontal line in your photo, and then rotate the photo so that this line is parallel to the nearest horizontal line in the grid. You can also match a vertical line in the photo with a vertical line in the grid.

Remove Red-Eye from a Photo

If you have a photo where one or more people or animals have red eyes due to the camera flash, you can use iPhoto to remove the red eye and give your subjects a more natural look.

① Click the photo that contains the red eye.

② Click **Edit**.

iPhoto displays its editing tools.

③ Click **Red-Eye** (⊗).

128

iPhoto displays its Red-Eye controls.

● If needed, you can click and drag this slider to the right to zoom in on the picture.

④ Click the red eye in the photo.

● iPhoto removes the red eye.

⑤ Repeat Step **4** to fix any other instances of red eye in the photo.

⑥ Click ⊗ (or click ⊚) to exit the Red-Eye tool.

⑦ Click **Done.**

iPhoto exits Edit mode.

Why does iPhoto not remove the red eye in my photo when I click it with the Red-Eye tool?

The red eye may not be "red" enough for iPhoto to automatically fix it. To work around this problem, you can use the manual version of the Red-Eye tool. Follow these steps:

① Follow Steps **1** to **3** to display the Red-Eye controls.

② In the **Size** list, click 🔽 and then click **Manual.**

③ Click and drag the slider until the displayed circle is the size of the red-eye area.

④ Use your mouse to move the circle over the red eye and then click.

iPhoto removes the red eye that occurs within the circle.

Enhance a Photo with an Effect

You can give a photo a more interesting look by applying an effect to the photo. iPhoto offers several different effects, including black and white or sepia coloring, fading or boosting the color, and edge blurring.

SEPIA EFFECT

Enhance a Photo with an Effect

① Click the photo that you want to enhance.

② Click **Edit.**

iPhoto displays its editing tools.

③ Click **Effects (▦).**

iPhoto displays the Effects palette.

④ Click the effect you want to apply.

● iPhoto applies the effect.

⑤ If the effect offers a numeric value, click the arrow buttons to set the value you prefer.

⑥ Repeat Steps **4** and **5** to apply other effects to the photo.

⑦ Click ⊗ (or click ▦) to exit the Effects tool.

⑧ Click **Done.**

iPhoto exits Edit mode.

TIPS

How do I remove an effect?

If it is an effect such as Sepia or Antique that does not have an associated numeric value, click the effect again to turn it off. For an effect that has a numeric value, reduce the value to 0. If you have already applied one or more effects, right-click the photo and then click **Revert to Original.**

I just want my photo to look better. Is there an easy way to do that?

Yes, there is. iPhoto comes with an Enhance tool that adjusts several photo elements to optimum values, including exposure, contrast, color saturation, and tint. Click the photo, click **Edit,** and then click **Enhance** ( ). If you are an experienced photographer, you can enhance the photo by hand by clicking **Adjust** ( ).

E-mail a Photo

If you have a photo that you want to share with someone, and you know that person's e-mail address, you can use iPhoto to send the photo in an e-mail message.

Even if a photo is very large, you can still send it via e-mail because you can use iPhoto to shrink the copy of the photo that appears in the message.

① Click the photo you want to send.

② Click **Share**.

③ Click **Email**.

● You can also click **Email** ().

The Mail Photo dialog box appears.

④ In the **Size** list, click 🔼 and then click the size you want to use for the sent photo.

⑤ Click **Compose.**

iPhoto creates a new Apple Mail message.

● The photo appears in the message body.

⑥ Use the To text box to type the address of the message recipient.

⑦ Use the Subject text box to type the message subject.

⑧ Click **Send.**

Apple Mail sends the message.

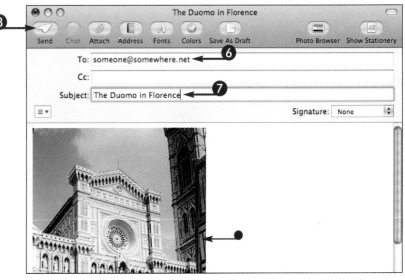

TIP

How do I insert some text above the photo?
Inserting a bit of text above the photo is a good idea because it enables you to introduce the photo and let the recipient know why you are sending it. To add the text, follow these steps:

① Click inside the narrow white area to the left of the photo.

Apple Mail displays a large, blinking cursor to the left of the photo.

② Press Return.

③ Press ⬆.

The cursor moves into the new line you created.

④ Type your message above the photo.

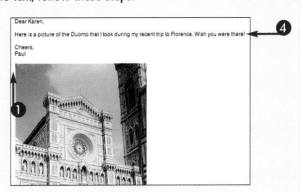

Take Your Picture

If your Mac comes with a built-in iSight camera, or if you have a third-party camera attached to your Mac, you can use the camera to take a picture of yourself using the Photo Booth application.

Once you have taken your picture, you can e-mail that picture, add it to iPhoto, or set is as your user account or iChat buddy picture.

Take Your Picture

TAKE YOUR PICTURE WITH PHOTO BOOTH

1 In the Dock, click 📷.

2 Click **Applications.**

3 Double-click **Photo Booth.**

● You can also click the Dock's **Photo Booth** icon (📷).

The Photo Booth window appears.

● The live feed from the camera appears here.

4 Click **Take a still picture** (▢).

● Click **Take four quick pictures** (⊞) if you want Photo Booth to snap four successive photos, each about 1 second apart.

● Click **Take a movie clip** (▤) if you want Photo Booth to capture the live camera feed as a movie.

5 Click **Take Photo** (⊙).

Note: *You can also press* ⌘+T *or click* **File** *and then click* **Take Photo.**

Photo Booth counts down 3 seconds and then takes the photo.

Note: *When the Mac is taking your picture, be sure to look into the camera, not into the screen.*

WORK WITH YOUR PHOTO BOOTH PICTURE

● Photo Booth displays the picture.

1 Click the taken picture.

● Click **Email** (🖼) to send the photo in an e-mail message.

● Click **iPhoto** (🖼) to add the photo to iPhoto.

● Click **Account Picture** (👥) to set the photo as your user account picture.

● Click **Buddy Picture** (🖼) to set the photo as your iChat buddy picture.

TIP

Is there some way to make my photos more interesting?

Definitely. Photo Booth comes with around two dozen special effects that can make your photo look like an X-ray or comic book, apply distortions such as a mirror image, add a background image, and more. Follow these steps:

1 In Photo Booth, click **Effects.**

2 Click an icon to select a different page of effects.

● You can also use the arrow buttons to change pages.

3 Click the effect you want to use.

You can create a slideshow of photos and burn it to a recordable DVD disc for playback on your Mac or on your home or portable DVD player. After you start the slideshow, the feature automatically advances and displays each photo on the disc as a slide.

Create a DVD of Your Photos

① In iPhoto, select the photos that you want to add to the DVD.

② Click **Share.**

③ Click **Send to iDVD.**

iDVD loads, starts a new project, and populates the project with the photos.

④ Click **Themes.**

⑤ Click the theme you want to use.

⑥ Double-click the menu title.

⑦ Use the pop-up menus to set the title font.

⑧ Type a new title and then press Return.

⑨ Click **Media.**

⑩ Click **Photos.**

⑪ Click and drag a photo and drop it on the theme's Drop Zone 1.

TIP

How do I remove the Apple logo from the main menu?

Follow these steps:

① Click **iDVD.**

② Click **Preferences.**

③ Click **General.**

④ Click **Show Apple logo watermark** (☑ changes to ☐).

⑤ Click 🔘.

continued

137

iDVD offers a number of options for displaying slideshow images. For example, you can change the duration that each image appears (the longer the duration, the fewer images you can place on the disc), and you can specify a transition effect between each image.

● iDVD displays the photo in the drop zone.

⑫ Double-click **Photos.**

● iDVD displays the slideshow editor.

⑬ To change the order in which the photos appear during the slideshow, click and drag a photo thumbnail and drop it in the new location.

⑭ To remove a photo from the slideshow, click the photo and then press Del.

⑮ In the Slide Duration pop-up menu, click ⬥ and then click the amount of time you want to see each photo.

⑯ In the Transition pop-up menu, click ⬥ and then click the type of transition you want to see between each photo.

⑰ Insert a blank recordable DVD into your Mac's DVD drive.

Note: *If you see a dialog box asking what you want to do with the blank DVD, click* ***Ignore.***

⑱ Click **File.**

⑲ Click **Burn DVD.**

Note: *You can also press* ⌘+R *or click the* ***Burn*** *button (⬚).*

   iDVD burns the photos to the DVD.

⑳ Click **Done.**

TIPS

How can I get my photos to play in a continuous loop?

In the iDVD window, follow Steps **12** and **13** to display the project's slideshow. Click **Settings** (⬚) and then click the **Loop slideshow** check box (⬚ changes to ✓). Click **OK** to put the new settings into effect.

Can I add a music soundtrack to my slideshow?

Yes. In the iDVD window, display the slideshow editor, click **Media,** and then click **Audio.** Locate the song you want to use. Click and drag the song from the **Audio** list and drop it on the audio icon (⬚). To remove the song, click and drag it from the audio icon and drop it outside of the audio icon.

CHAPTER 7

Creating a Movie

Your Mac comes with the tools you need to create your own digital video movies. You can import camcorder video, apply scene transitions, add titles, credits, and a soundtrack, and even export your movie to a DVD.

Open and Close iMovie

Your Mac includes iMovie to enable you to import video from a digital camcorder, view videos, and create your own movies. To begin using the program, you must first learn how to find and open the iMovie window. When you finish using the program, you can close the iMovie window to free up computer-processing power.

Open and Close iMovie

OPEN IMOVIE

① Click [icon] in the Dock.

② Click **Applications**.

③ Double-click **iMovie**.

The first time you launch iMovie, the program tells you that it must generate video thumbnails.

Note: *You see this dialog box only if your Mac has at least one digital video file.*

④ Click **Now**.

The iMovie window appears.

CLOSE IMOVIE

① Click **iMovie**.

② Click **Quit iMovie**.

TIPS

Are there faster methods I can use to open iMovie?

The fastest way to start iMovie is to click the iMovie icon ( ) in the Dock. If you have used iMovie recently, another reasonably fast method is to click the **Apple icon** ( ), click **Recent Items,** and then click **iMovie.**

Are there faster methods I can use to close iMovie?

Probably the fastest method you can use to quit iMovie is to click . Alternatively, Ctrl+click or right-click   and then click **Quit.** Finally, if your hands are closer to the keyboard than to the mouse, you can quit iMovie by pressing ⌘+Q.

Import a Video File

If you have video content on a FireWire digital camcorder, you can connect the camcorder to your Mac and then import some or all of the video to your iMovie project.

See Chapter 3 to learn how to connect a digital camcorder to your Mac.

Import a Video File

IMPORT ALL FOOTAGE

① Connect the digital camcorder to your Mac.

iMovie displays its Import From window.

② Click **Import.**

iMovie rewinds the tape to the beginning, imports all the footage, and then rewinds the tape.

iMovie prompts you to create a new event.

③ Use the Create new Event text box to type a name for the import event.

④ Click **OK.**

IMPORT SELECTED FOOTAGE

① Connect the digital camcorder to your Mac.

iMovie displays its Import From window.

② Click **Manual.**

③ Click **Play** (▶).

● You can click and hold **Seek Forward** (▶▶) to speed up the playback.

● If you go too far, you can click and hold **Seek Back** (◀◀) to skip back.

④ When you get to the part you want to import, click **Import.**

iMovie pauses the playback and prompts you to create a new event.

⑤ Use the Create new Event text box to type a name for the import event.

⑥ Click **OK.**

iMovie restarts the tape and begins importing the video.

*Note: To skip recording some of the tape, click **Stop** and then repeat Steps **3** to **6**. In the dialog box, be sure to click **Add to existing Event** (○ changes to ⊙).*

⑦ Click **Done.**

 TIP

How do I import digital video from my iSight camera?
Follow these steps:

① In iMovie, click **File.**

② Click **Import from Camera.**

③ In the **Video Size** pop-up menu, click ⬍ and then click the frame size you want.

④ Click **Capture.**

⑤ Follow Steps **5** and **6** on this page.

⑥ When you are done, click **Stop.**

⑦ Click **Done.**

Add Video Clips to Your Project

A *video clip* is a segment of digital video. You begin building your movie by adding one or more video clips to your project.

When you import digital video as described in the previous section, iMovie automatically breaks up the video into separate clips.

Add Video Clips to Your Project

ADD AN ENTIRE CLIP

① Click the Library item that contains the video clip you want to add.

② Press and hold the `Option` key and click the clip.

● iMovie selects the entire clip.

③ Click and drag the selected clip and drop it in your project at the spot where you want the clip to appear.

● iMovie adds the entire video clip to the project.

ADD A PARTIAL CLIP

1. Click the Library item that contains the video clip you want to add.

2. Click the clip at the point where you want the selection to begin.

3. Click and drag the right edge of the selection box to the point where you want the selection to end.

4. Click and drag the selected clip and drop it in your project at the spot where you want the clip to appear.

● iMovie adds the selected portion of the video clip to the project.

Is it possible to play a clip before I add it?

Sure. The easiest way to do this is to double-click the clip at the point where you want the playback to start. iMovie plays the clip in the playback area in the top-right corner of the window. Click the clip to stop the playback. If you want to see only a portion of the clip, follow Steps **2** and **3** on this page to make your selection, `Ctrl` +click or right-click the clip and then click **Play Selection.**

I added a clip in the wrong place. Can I move it?

Yes. In your project, click the added clip to select it. Use your mouse (⟍) to click and drag the clip and then drop the clip in the correct location within the project. If you want to delete the clip from the project, click it, click **Edit,** and then click **Delete Entire Clip.**

If you have a video clip that is too long or contains footage you do not need, you can shorten the clip or remove the extra footage. Removing parts of a video clip is called *trimming* the clip.

Trim a Clip

① In your project, click the clip you want to trim.

● iMovie selects the entire clip.

② Use your mouse (➤) to click and drag the left edge of the selection box to the starting position of the part of the clip you want to keep.

③ Use your mouse (➤) to click and drag the right edge of the selection box to the ending position of the part of the clip you want to keep.

4 Click **Edit.**

5 Click **Trim to Selection.**

Note: You can also press ⌘ *+* B *.*

● iMovie trims the clip.

TIP

Is it possible to trim a certain number of frames from a clip?

Yes, iMovie enables you to trim up to 30 frames (1 second) at a time from either the beginning or the end of the clip. Follow these steps:

1 Position the mouse (▶) over the clip you want to trim.

2 To trim from the beginning, click **Fine Tune Clip** (◀▶) near the beginning of the clip.

To trim from the end, click ◀▶ near the end of the clip, instead.

3 Use your mouse (▶) to click and drag the edge of the selection box.

● iMovie displays the number of frames you are trimming.

4 Release the mouse (▶) when you reach the number of frames that you want to trim.

Add a Transition Between Clips

By default, iMovie jumps immediately from the end of one clip to the beginning of another. You can add more visual interest to your movie by adding a transition between the two clips.

iMovie offers a dozen different transitions, including various fades, wipes, and dissolves.

Add a Transition Between Clips

1 Click the **Transitions browser** button (⬛).

● iMovie displays the available transitions.

Note: To see a preview of a transition, position your mouse (🖢) over the transition thumbnail.

2 Use your mouse (🖢) to click and drag a transition and drop it between the two clips.

● iMovie adds an icon for the transition between the two clips.

③ Position your mouse (k) over the transition.

● iMovie displays a preview of the transition.

TIP

Can I change the duration of the transition?
Yes. The default length is half a second, but you can increase or decrease the duration by following these steps:

① Click the transition icon in your project.

② Click **Edit**.

③ Click **Set Duration** (or press ⌘+R).

④ Use the Duration text box to set the number of seconds you want the transition to take.

⑤ If you want to change only the current transition, click **Applies only to selected transition** (○ changes to ⊙).

⑥ Click **OK.**

Although most movie projects consist of several video clips, you can also add a photo to your project. By default, iMovie displays the photo for 4 seconds.

You can also specify how the photo fits in the movie frame: You can adjust the size of the photo to fit the frame, you can crop the photo, or you can apply a Ken Burns effect to animate the static photo.

Add a Photo

① Click the **Photos browser** button (📷).

● iMovie displays the available photos.

② Click and drag a photo and drop it inside your project.

● iMovie adds the photo to the movie.

③ Click the **Crop** button (🔲).

- iMovie displays the cropping options for the photo.

④ Click **Ken Burns.**

- You can also click **Fit** to have iMovie adjust the size of the photo to fit the movie frame.

- You can also click **Crop** and then click and drag the cropping rectangle to specify how much of the photo you want to appear in the movie frame.

⑤ Click and drag the green rectangle to set the start point of the Ken Burns animation.

⑥ Click and drag the red rectangle to set the end point of the Ken Burns animation.

Note: Click and drag the corners and edges of the rectangle to change the size; click and drag the interior of the rectangles to change the position.

⑦ Click **Done.**

TIP

Can I change the length of time that the photo appears in the movie?

Yes. The default length is 4 seconds, but you can increase or decrease the duration by following these steps:

① Click the photo in your project.

② Click **Edit.**

③ Click **Set Duration** (or press ⌘+ℝ).

④ Use the Duration text box to set the number of seconds you want the photo to appear.

⑤ If you want to change the duration for all photos, click **Applies to all photos** (◯ changes to ◉).

⑥ Click **OK.**

Add a Music Track

You can enhance the audio component of your movie by adding one or more songs that play in the background.

To get the best audio experience, you can adjust various sound properties, including the volume of the music clip, the volume of the video clip, and how the song clip fades in and out.

Add a Music Track

① Click the **Music and Sound Effects browser** button (♫).

● iMovie displays the available audio files.

② Use your mouse (➤) to click and drag a song and drop it inside your project.

● iMovie adds the song to the movie.

③ Click the music clip to select it.

Note: *iMovie treats the song like a clip, which means you can trim the song as needed, as described earlier in the "Trim a Clip" section.*

④ Click the **Adjust Audio** button (◄◄).

iMovie displays the Audio Adjustments dialog box.

⑤ Use the Volume slider to adjust the volume of the music clip.

⑥ If you want to reduce the video clip volume, click **Ducking** (☐ changes to ☑) and then click and drag the slider.

⑦ To adjust the fade-in time, click **Fade In: Manual** (◯ changes to ◉) and then click and drag the slider.

⑧ To adjust the fade-out time, click **Fade Out: Manual** (◯ changes to ◉) and then click and drag the slider.

⑨ Click **Done**.

When I add a video clip before the music clip, the music does not play with the new video clip. How can I work around this?

You need to add your song as a background track instead of a clip. Here are the steps to follow:

① Click 🎵.

② Use your mouse (k) to click and drag a song.

③ Drop the song on the project background, not on a clip or between two clips.

● The background turns green when you have the song positioned correctly.

You can add multiple background tracks, and then click **Edit** and **Arrange Music Tracks** to reorder them. To pin a music track to a particular video clip, click and drag the song title to the beginning of the video clip.

Record a Voiceover

You can augment the audio portion of your movie by recording a voiceover. A voiceover is useful for explaining a video clip, introducing the movie, or giving the viewer background information about the movie.

To record a voiceover, your Mac must either have a built-in microphone or an external microphone connected either via the Line In jack, USB port, or Bluetooth.

Record a Voiceover

① If your Mac does not have a built-in microphone, attach a microphone.

*Note: You may need to configure the microphone as the sound input device. Click [icon], click **Sound**, click **Input**, and then click your microphone.*

② Click the **Voiceover** button ([icon]).

The Voiceover dialog box appears.

③ Click the spot in the movie at which you want the voiceover to begin.

iMovie counts down and then begins the recording.

④ Speak your voiceover text into the microphone.

⑤ When you are finished, click **Recording.**

● iMovie adds the voiceover to the clip.

⑥ Click **Close** (☒).

● You can click to adjust the voiceover audio, as described in the previous task.

TIP

Is there a way to tell if my voice is too loud or too soft?

Yes, you can use the controls in the Voiceover dialog box. You check your voice level by talking into the microphone and then watching the Left and Right volume meters:

● If you see no green bars or just a few green bars, your voice level is too low.

● If you see yellow or red bars, your voice level is too high.

Use the Input Volume slider to adjust the voice level up or down, as needed.

Add Titles and Credits

You can get your movie off to a proper start by adding a title and a subtitle. iMovie offers a number of title styles that you can choose from. You can also enhance your movie with scrolling credits at the end.

① Click the **Titles browser** button (T).

- iMovie displays the available title types.

② Use your mouse (k) to click and drag a title and drop it where you want the titles to appear.

Note: To see just the titles, drop the title thumbnail at the beginning of the movie or between two clips. To superimpose the titles on a video clip, drop the title thumbnail on the clip.

- If you want to add credits, click and drag the **Scrolling Credits** thumbnail and drop it at the end of the movie.

● iMovie adds a clip for the titles.

③ Replace this text with the movie title.

④ Replace this text with the movie subtitle.

⑤ Click **Done.**

Note: *iMovie treats the title like a clip, which means you can lengthen or shorten the title duration by clicking and dragging the beginning or end, as described earlier in the "Trim a Clip" section.*

TIP

How do I change the font of the titles?
The Text menu offers several font-related commands, including Bold, Italic, Bigger, and Smaller. You can also click the **Show Fonts** command to display the Fonts dialog box.

Play the Movie

While you are building your iMovie project, it is a good idea to occasionally play some or all of the movie to make sure the video and audio are working properly and the transitions appear when you want them to.

Play the Movie

PLAY FROM THE BEGINNING

1 Click **View**.

2 Click **Play from Beginning**.

Note: You can also press \ or click the Play Project from beginning button (▶).

PLAY FROM A SPECIFIC LOCATION

1 Click the spot where you want to start playing the movie.

2 Click **View**.

3 Click **Play**.

Note: You can also press Spacebar or double-click the movie location.

PLAY A SELECTION

① Select the video clips you want to play.

Note: See the Tip below to learn how to select multiple video clips.

② Click **View.**

③ Click **Play Selection.**

Note: You can also press /.

TIPS

How do I select multiple video clips?

To select multiple video clips, press and hold ⌘ and then click anywhere inside each clip you want to select. If you select a clip by accident, ⌘+click again to deselect it. If you want to skip just a few clips, first press ⌘+A to select all the clips. Then press and hold ⌘ and click the clips you do not want in the selection.

Can I enlarge the size of the playback window?

Yes, you can play your movie in full-screen mode. To do this, click **View** and then click **Play Full Screen.** You can also press ⌘+G or click the **Play Project full screen** button (▶).

Create a DVD of Your Movie

When your movie project is complete, you can burn it to a recordable DVD disc for playback on your Mac or on your home or portable DVD player.

Creating a DVD requires three separate procedures: exporting your iMovie project to a QuickTime video file, importing that video file into iDVD, and then burning the DVD project to disc.

Create a DVD of Your Movie

EXPORT TO A QUICKTIME VIDEO FILE

1 In iMovie, click **Share.**

2 Click **Export using QuickTime.**

The Save Exported File As dialog box appears.

3 Use the Save As text box to type a name for the exported movie file.

4 Click **Save.**

iMovie exports the project to a QuickTime file.

Note: *Depending on the length of your movie and the number of transitions, music tracks, and other options, it may take an hour or more to export the movie.*

IMPORT THE VIDEO FILE TO THE DVD PROJECT

1 In the Dock, click **iDVD** ().

2 Click **Add** (➕).

3 Click **Add Movie**.

● iDVD adds a button for the movie.

4 Click **Media**.

5 Click **Movies**.

6 Click and drag the movie thumbnail and drop it on the **Add Movie Here** button.

iDVD adds the movie to the DVD project.

TIP

Is there any way to set up the DVD so that my movie starts as soon as I insert the disc?

Yes, by following these steps:

1 Click **Show the DVD Map** (🔲).

2 Click and drag your movie and drop it on the map's first box.

iDVD moves the movie to the beginning of the DVD.

3 Click 🔲 to return to the main screen.

continued

You can customize your DVD by choosing a theme, modifying the menu title, and adding a photo to the theme's drop zone.

Create a DVD of Your Movie *(continued)*

CREATE THE DVD

❶ Click **Themes.**

❷ Click the theme you want to use.

*Note: If iDVD displays the Change Project Aspect Ratio dialog box, click **Change.***

❸ Double-click the menu title.

❹ Use the pop-up menus to set the title font.

❺ Type a new title and then press Return.

❻ Click **Media.**

❼ Click **Photos.**

❽ Click and drag a photo and drop it on the theme's Drop Zone 1.

iDVD displays the photo in the drop zone.

9 Insert a blank recordable DVD into your Mac's DVD drive.

Note: If you see a dialog box asking what you want to do with the blank DVD, click Ignore.

10 Click **File.**

11 Click **Burn DVD.**

Note: You can also press ⌘ + R or click the Burn button ( ).

iDVD burns the movie to the DVD.

12 Click **Done.**

How can I display a still from my movie in the main menu?

Follow these steps:

1 Follow Steps **6** to **8** on the previous page, except click Movies instead of Photos, and drag and drop your movie on the drop zone.

2 Click and drag the **Movie Start** bar until you see the frame you want to use.

3 Click and drag the **Movie End** bar until it is flush with the Movie Start bar.

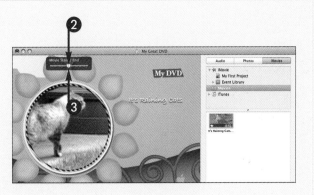

Surfing the World Wide Web

If your Mac is connected to the Internet either directly or through a network connection, you can use the Safari Web browser application to navigate — or *surf* — the sites of the World Wide Web. This chapter shows you how to navigate from site to site and how to make surfing the Web easier.

Open and Close Safari

Your Mac includes the Safari application to enable you to surf Web sites when your Mac is connected to the Internet. You can also use Safari to save your favorite sites and navigate your surfing history.

OPEN SAFARI

1 Click **Finder** (🔲) in the Dock.

2 Click **Applications.**

3 Double-click **Safari.**

The Safari window appears.

CLOSE SAFARI

① Click **Safari.**

② Click **Quit Safari.**

TIPS

Are there faster methods I can use to open Safari?

The fastest way to start Safari is to click the Safari icon (🧭) in the Dock. If you have used Safari recently, another reasonably fast method is to click 🍎, click **Recent Items,** and then click **Safari.**

Are there faster methods I can use to close Safari?

Probably the fastest method you can use to quit Safari is to Ctrl +click or right-click 🧭 and then click **Quit.** Finally, if your hands are closer to the keyboard than to the mouse, you can quit Safari by pressing ⌘+Q.

Select a Link

Almost all Web pages include links to other pages that contain information related to something in the current page, and you can use these links to navigate to other Web pages. When you select a link, your Web browser loads the other page.

Knowing which words, phrases, or images are links is not always obvious. The only way to tell for sure in many cases is to position the mouse (▶) over the text or image; if the ▶ changes to 🖑, you know you are dealing with a link.

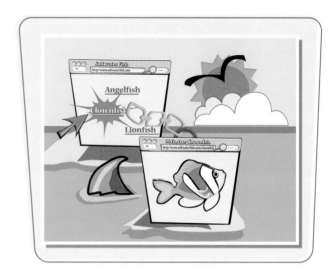

Select a Link

1 Position ▶ over the link (▶ changes to 🖑).

2 Click the text or image.

● The status bar shows the address of the page that the link will take you to.

Note: *The address shown in the status bar when you point at a link may be different than the one shown when the page is downloading. This occurs when the Web site "redirects" the link, which happens frequently.*

The linked Web page appears.

● The status bar shows the current download status.

● The Web page title and address change after the linked page is loaded.

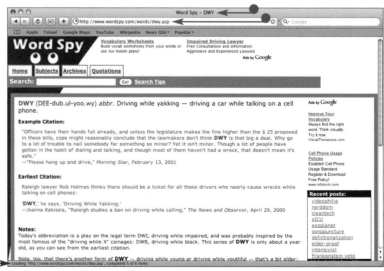

Enter a Web Page Address

If you know the address of a specific Web page, you can type it into the Web browser and the program displays the page.

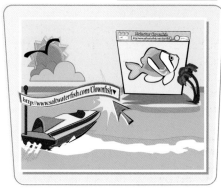

Enter a Web Page Address

1 Click inside the address bar.

2 Press Del to delete the existing address.

3 Type the address of the Web page you want to visit.

4 Press Return.

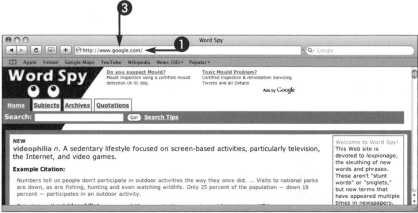

The Web page appears.

● The Web page title changes after the page is loaded.

Open a Web Page in a Tab

You can make it easier to work with multiple Web pages and sites simultaneously by opening each page in its own tab.

You can open as many pages as you want in their own tabs. This is convenient because all the pages appear within a single Safari window.

Open a Web Page in a Tab

OPEN A LINK IN A NEW TAB

① [Ctrl] +click or right-click the link you want to open.

② Click **Open Link in New Tab**.

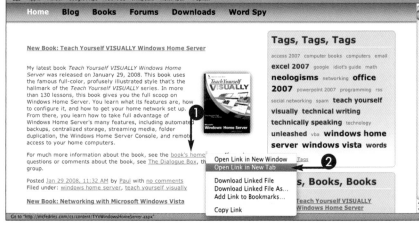

● A new tab appears with the page title.

③ Click the tab to display the page.

CREATE A NEW TAB

1 Click **File**.

2 Click **New Tab**.

● Safari creates a new tab.

3 Type the address of the page you want to load into the new tab.

4 Press Return.

Safari displays the page in the tab.

Are there any shortcuts I can use to open Web pages in tabs?

Here are some useful keyboard techniques:

● Press and hold ⌘ and click a link to open the page in a tab.

● Press and hold ⌘+Shift and click a link to open the page in a tab and display the tab.

● Type an address and then press ⌘+Return to open the page in a new tab.

● Type an address and then press Shift+⌘+Return to open the page in a new foreground tab.

● Press Shift+⌘+] or Shift+Ctrl+[to cycle through the tabs.

● Press ⌘+W to close the current tab.

● Press Option and click ⊠ to close every tab but the one you clicked.

Navigate Web Pages

After you have visited several pages, you can return to a page you visited earlier. Instead of retyping the address or looking for the link, Safari gives you some easier methods.

When you navigate Web pages, you can go back to a page you have visited in the current browser session. After you have done that, you can also reverse course and go forward through the pages again.

Navigate Web Pages

GO BACK ONE PAGE

① Click the **Previous Page** icon (◄).

The previous page you visited appears.

GO BACK SEVERAL PAGES

① Click and hold down ▸ on ◄.

A list of the pages you have visited appears.

② Click the page you want to display.

The page appears.

GO FORWARD ONE PAGE

1 Click the **Next Page** icon (▶).

The next page you visited appears.

Note: *If you are at the last page viewed up to that point, ▶ is not active.*

GO FORWARD SEVERAL PAGES

1 Click and hold down ▸ on ▶.

A list of the pages you have visited appears.

2 Click the page you want to display.

The page appears.

 TIP

Are there any shortcuts I can use to navigate Web pages?

Yes, there are a few useful keyboard shortcuts you can use:

- Press ⌘+[to go back one page.
- Press ⌘+] to go forward one page.
- Press Shift+⌘+H to return to the Safari home page (the first page you see when you open Safari).

Navigate with the History List

The Previous Page and Next Page buttons (◄ and ►) enable you to navigate pages only in the current browser session. To redisplay sites that you have visited in the past few days or weeks, you need to use the History list.

If you visit sensitive places such as an Internet banking site or your corporate site, you can increase security by clearing the History list so that other people cannot see where you have been.

Navigate with the History List

LOAD A PAGE FROM THE HISTORY LIST

① Click **History.**

② Click the date when you visited the page.

A list of pages that you visited during that day appears.

③ Click the page you want to display.

● The page appears.

CLEAR THE HISTORY LIST

① Click **History**.

② Click **Clear History**.

Safari deletes all the pages from the History list.

TIP

Can I control the length of time that Safari keeps track of the pages I visit?

Yes, by following these steps:

① In the menu bar, click **Safari.**

② Click **Preferences.**

③ Click **General.**

④ In the Remove history items pop-up menu, click 🛅 and then click the amount of time you want Safari to track your history.

⑤ Click 🔘.

Change Your Home Page

Your home page is the Web page that appears when you first start Safari. The default home page is usually the Apple.com Start page, but you can change that to any other page you want.

Safari also comes with a command that enables you to view the home page at any time during your browsing session.

CHANGE THE HOME PAGE

1 Display the Web page that you want to use as your home page.

2 Click **Safari.**

3 Click **Preferences.**

④ Click **General.**

⑤ Click **Set to Current Page.**

● Safari inserts the address of the current page in the Home page text box.

Note: If your Mac is not currently connected to the Internet, you can also type the new home page address manually using the Home page text box.

⑥ Click ▣.

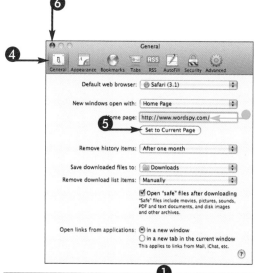

VIEW THE HOME PAGE

① Click **History.**

② Click **Home.**

Note: You can also display the home page by pressing Shift + ⌘ + H.

Safari displays the home page.

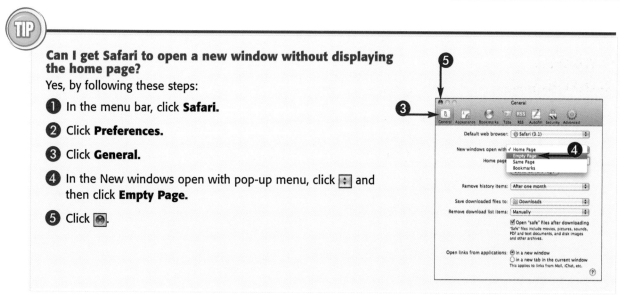

TIP

Can I get Safari to open a new window without displaying the home page?

Yes, by following these steps:

① In the menu bar, click **Safari.**

② Click **Preferences.**

③ Click **General.**

④ In the New windows open with pop-up menu, click ▣ and then click **Empty Page.**

⑤ Click ▣.

Bookmark Web Pages

If you have Web pages that you visit frequently, you can save yourself time by saving those pages as bookmarks within Safari. This enables you to display the pages with just a couple of mouse clicks.

In Safari, the Bookmarks bar appears just below the address bar. You can put your favorite sites on the Bookmarks bar for easiest access.

Bookmark Web Pages

BOOKMARK A WEB PAGE

① Display the Web page you want to save as a bookmark.

② Click **Bookmarks.**

③ Click **Add Bookmark.**

The Add Bookmark dialog box appears.

Note: *You can also display the Add Bookmark dialog box by pressing* ⌘ *+* D.

④ Edit the page name, as necessary.

⑤ Click ⟡ and then click the location where you want to store the bookmark.

⑥ Click **Add.**

Safari adds a bookmark for the page.

DISPLAY A BOOKMARKED WEB PAGE

① Click the **Show all bookmarks** button (📖).

● If you added the bookmark to the Bookmarks bar, click the page name.

● If you added the bookmark to a folder, click the folder and then click the page name.

The Bookmarks window appears.

② Click ▶ to open the folder that contains the bookmark you want (▶ changes to ▼).

③ Double-click the bookmark.

The Web page appears.

TIPS

I use my Bookmarks bar a lot. Is there an easier way to display these pages?

Yes, there is. Safari automatically assigns keyboard shortcuts to the first nine bookmarks, counting from left to right and not including folders. For example, you display the leftmost bookmark by pressing ⌘+**1**. Moving to the right, the shortcuts are ⌘+**2**, ⌘+**3**, and so on.

How do I delete a bookmark?

If the site is on the Bookmarks bar, **Ctrl**+click or right-click the bookmark and then click **Delete.** For all other bookmarks, click 📖 to display the Bookmarks window. Locate the bookmark you want to remove, **Ctrl**+click or right-click the bookmark, and then click **Delete.** You can also click the bookmark and then press **Del**.

Search for Sites

If you need information on a specific topic, Safari has a built-in feature that enables you to quickly search the Web for sites that have the information you require.

The Web has a number of sites called *search engines* that enable you to find what you are looking for. By default, Safari uses the Google search site (www.google.com).

Search for Sites

① Click in the search box.

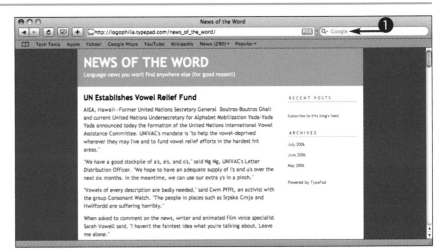

② Type a word, phrase, or question that represents the information you want to find.

③ Press **Return**.

● A list of pages that match your search text appears.

④ Click a Web page.

The page appears.

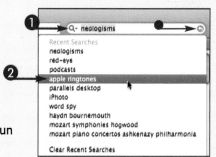

Download a File

Some Web sites make files available for you to open on your Mac. To use these files, you must first download them to your Mac using Safari.

To use a file from a Web site, you must have an application designed to work with that particular file type. For example, if the file is an Excel workbook, you need either Excel for the Mac or a compatible program.

Download a File

1 Navigate to the page that contains the link to the file.

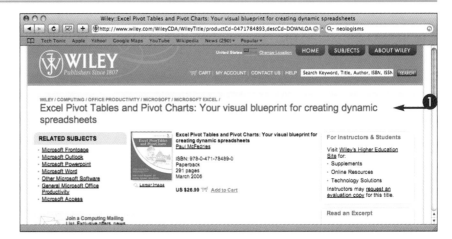

2 Click the link to the file.

Safari downloads the file to your Mac.

- The Downloads window shows the progress of the download.

3 When the download is complete, `Ctrl`+click or right-click the file.

4 Click **Open.**

The file opens in the corresponding application.

TIP

How do I remove items from my Downloads window?

Follow these steps:

1 In Safari, click **Window.**

2 Click **Downloads.**

The Downloads window appears.

You can also display the Downloads window by pressing `Option`+`⌘`+`L`.

3 `Ctrl`+click or right-click the downloaded file you want to remove.

4 Click **Remove From List.**

- If you want to delete the downloaded file itself, click **Show in Finder** (🔍) and then delete the file from the Downloads folder.

Communicating via E-mail and Chat

You can use the Apple Mail application to send e-mail to and read e-mail from friends, family, colleagues, and even total strangers almost anywhere in the world. You can also use the iChat application to exchange instant messages. This chapter shows you how to perform these and many more communications tasks.

Open and Close Mail

Your Mac includes the Apple Mail application to enable you to use an e-mail account to exchange and manage e-mail messages. Before you can send or receive e-mail messages, you must know how to start the Mail application.

OPEN MAIL

① Click **Finder** (🖼️) in the Dock.

② Click **Applications.**

③ Double-click the Mail icon (📧).

Note: *If the Welcome to Mail dialog box appears, see the next task to learn how to set up your first e-mail account in Mail.*

The Mail window appears.

CLOSE MAIL

1 Click **Mail.**

2 Click **Quit Mail.**

TIPS

Are there faster methods I can use to open Mail?

The fastest way to start Mail is to click the Mail icon ( ) in the Dock. If you have used Mail recently, another reasonably fast method is to click , click **Recent Items,** and then click **Mail.**

Are there faster methods I can use to close Mail?

Probably the fastest method you can use to quit Mail is to Ctrl +click or right-click   and then click **Quit.** If your hands are closer to the keyboard than to the mouse, you can quit Mail by pressing + .

Add an E-mail Account

Before you can send an e-mail message, you must add your e-mail account to the Mail application. This also enables you to use Mail to retrieve the messages that others have sent to your account.

Your e-mail account is usually a POP (Post Office Protocol) account supplied by your Internet service provider, which should have supplied you with the POP account details. You can also set up Mail with your MobileMe account, if you have one.

Add an E-mail Account

GET STARTED ADDING AN ACCOUNT

① Click **File**.

② Click **Add Account.**

Note: If you are just starting Mail and the Welcome to Mail dialog box is on-screen, you can skip Steps 1 and 2.

The Add Account dialog box appears. If you are starting Mail for the first time, the Welcome to Mail dialog box is identical.

ADD A MOBILEME ACCOUNT

① Use the Full Name text box to type your name.

② Use the Email Address text box to type your MobileMe account address.

③ Use the Password text box to type your MobileMe account password.

④ Click **Automatically set up account** (☐ changes to ☑).

⑤ Click **Create**.

Mail adds your MobileMe account.

ADD A POP ACCOUNT

❶ Use the Full Name text box to type your name.

❷ Use the Email Address text box to type your POP account address.

❸ Use the Password text box to type your POP account password. Click **Continue.**

❹ In the Account Type list, click ⬍ and then click **POP.**

❺ Use the Description text box to describe the account.

❻ Use the Incoming Mail Server text box to type the address of the account's incoming mail server.

Note: The incoming mail server is also sometimes called the POP or POPD server.

❼ Edit the User Name text as required. Click **Continue.**

❽ Type a Description of the outgoing mail server.

❾ Type the address of the Outgoing Mail Server.

Note: The outgoing mail server is also sometimes called the SMTP server.

● If your ISP requires authentication, click **Use Authentication** (☐ changes to ☑).

❿ Click **Continue**. Click **Continue** again. Click **Create.**

TIP

My e-mail account requires me to use a nonstandard outgoing mail port. How do I set this up?

Follow these steps:

❶ In the menu bar, click **Mail.**

❷ Click **Preferences.**

❸ Click **Accounts.**

❹ In the Outgoing Mail Server (SMTP) list, click ⬍ and then click **Edit Server List.**

❺ Click the outgoing mail server.

❻ Click **Advanced.**

❼ Use the Server port text box to type the nonstandard port number.

❽ Click **OK.**

❾ Click ⬛.

❿ Click **Save.**

Send an E-mail Message

If you know the e-mail address of a person or organization, you can send an e-mail message to that address. In most cases, the message is delivered within a few minutes.

If you do not know any e-mail addresses, or if at first you prefer to just practice sending messages, you can send messages to your own e-mail address.

① Click **New Message.**

Note: You can also start a new message by pressing ⌘ + N.

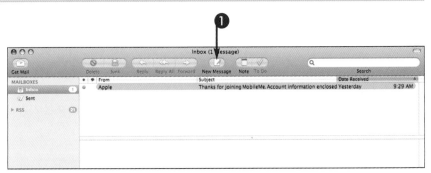

A message window appears.

② Use the To field to type the e-mail address of the person to whom you are sending the message.

③ To send a copy of the message to another person, use the Cc field to type that person's e-mail address.

Note: You can add multiple e-mail addresses in both the To line and the Cc line. Separate each address with a comma (,).

④ Use the Subject field to type a title or short description for the message.

5 Type the message.

● To change the message font, you can click **Fonts** to display the Fonts dialog box.

● To change the text colors, you can click **Colors** to display the Color palette.

● To change the overall look of the message, click **Show Stationery** and then click a theme.

*Note: Many people use e-mail programs that cannot process text formatting. Unless you are sure your recipient's program supports formatting, it is best to send plain-text messages. To do this, click **Format** and then click **Make Plain Text.***

6 Click **Send.**

Mail sends your message.

Note: Mail stores a copy of your message in the Sent folder.

I have a large number of messages to compose. Do I have to be online to do this?

No, composing all the messages while you are offline is possible. Follow these steps:

1 While disconnected from the Internet, start Mail.

2 To ensure you are working offline, click **Mailbox.** If the **Take All Accounts Offline** command is enabled, click that command.

3 Compose and send the message. Each time you click **Send,** your message is stored temporarily in the Outbox folder.

4 When you are done, connect to the Internet.

After a few moments, Mail automatically sends all the messages sitting in the Outbox folder.

Add a File Attachment

If you have a memo, photo, or other document that you want to send to another person, you can attach the document to an e-mail message. The other person can then open the document after he or she receives your message.

1 Click **New Message.**

A message window appears.

2 Click **Attach.**

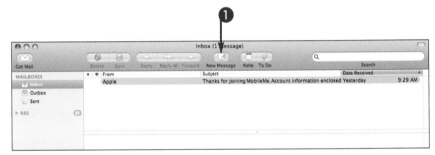

A file selection dialog box appears.

③ Click the file you want to attach.

④ Click **Choose File.**

● Mail attaches the file to the message.

Note: Another way to attach a file to a message is to click and drag the file from Finder and drop it inside the message.

⑤ Repeat Steps **2** to **4** to attach additional files to the message.

⑥ Fill in the rest of the fields and then send your message as described in the previous section.

Is there a limit to the number of files I can attach to a message?

There is no practical limit to the number of files you can attach to the message. However, you should be careful with the total *size* of the files you send. If you or the recipient has a slow Internet connection, sending or receiving the message can take an extremely long time. Also, many ISPs place a limit on the size of a message's attachments, which is usually between 2MB and 5MB. In general, use e-mail to send only a few small files at a time.

Add a Signature

In an e-mail message, a *signature* is a small amount of text that appears at the bottom of the message. Rather than typing this information manually in each message, you can create the signature once and then have Mail automatically add the signature to any message you send.

Signatures usually contain personal contact information, such as your phone number, business address, and e-mail and Web site addresses. Some people supplement their signatures with wise or witty quotations.

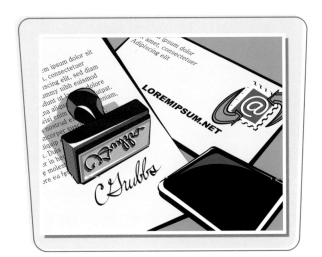

Add a Signature

CREATE A SIGNATURE

1. Click **Mail**.

2. Click **Preferences**.

The Mail preferences appear.

3. Click **Signatures**.

4. Click the account for which you want to use the signature.

5. Click **Create a signature** (+).

Mail adds a new signature.

6 Type a name for the signature.

7 Type the signature text.

8 Repeat Steps **4** to **7** to add other signatures, if required.

Note: You can add as many signatures as you want. For example, you may want to have one signature for business use and another for personal use.

9 Click .

INSERT THE SIGNATURE

1 Click **New Message** to start a new message.

Note: To see how to start a new message, refer to the section "Send an E-mail Message" earlier in this chapter.

2 In the message text area, move the insertion point to the location where you want the signature to appear.

3 In the Signature pop-up menu, click ⬍ and then click the signature you want to insert.

● The signature appears in the message.

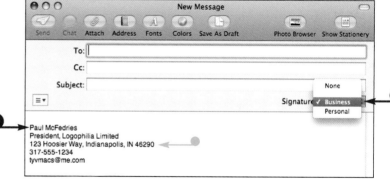

TIP

Can I get Mail to add my signature automatically?

Yes, by following these steps:

1 Follow Steps **1** to **4** to display the signature preferences and choose an account.

2 In the **Choose Signature** pop-up menu, click ⬍ and then click the signature you want to insert automatically into each message.

3 Click **Place signature above quoted text** (☐ changes to ☑).

If you prefer that your signature appear at the very bottom of your replies and forwards, turn off the **Place signature above quoted text** check box (☑ changes to ☐).

4 Click .

Receive and Read E-mail Messages

A message sent to you by another person is stored on your ISP's e-mail server computer. You must connect to the ISP's computer to retrieve and read the message. As you see in this section, Mail does most of the work for you automatically.

Mail checks for new messages when you start the program automatically, and then checks for more messages every 5 minutes while you are online.

Receive and Read E-mail Messages

RECEIVE E-MAIL MESSAGES

① Click **Get Mail**.

● The Mail Activity area lets you know if you have any incoming messages.

● If you have new messages, they appear in your Inbox folder with a blue dot in this column.

● Messages from Apple appear in your Inbox folder with a blue background.

● The 🖾 icon in the Dock shows the number of unread messages in the Inbox folder.

READ A MESSAGE

1 Click the message.

2 Read the message text in the preview pane.

Note: If you want to open the message in its own window, double-click the message.

TIP

Can I change how often Mail automatically checks for messages?

Yes, by following these steps:

1 Click **Mail.**

2 Click **Preferences.**

The Mail preferences appear.

3 Click the **General** tab.

4 In the **Check for new mail pop-up** menu, click 🔽 and then click the time interval that you want Mail to use when checking for new messages automatically.

● If you do not want Mail to check for messages automatically, click **Manually,** instead.

5 Click 🔘.

Reply to a Message

When a message you receive requires some kind of response — whether it is answering a question, supplying information, or providing comments or criticisms — you can send a reply to the person who sent that message.

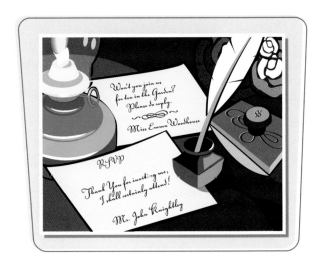

1 Click the message to which you want to reply.

2 Click the reply type you want to use.

Click **Reply** to respond only to the first address displayed on the message's To line.

Click **Reply All** to respond to all the addresses in the message's To and Cc lines.

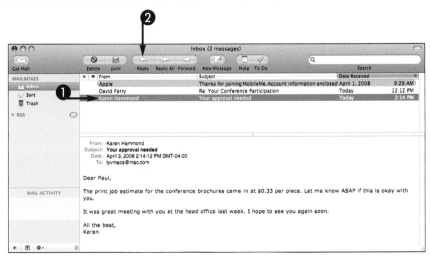

A message window appears.

● Mail automatically inserts the recipient addresses.

● Mail also inserts the subject line, preceded by Re:.

● Mail includes the original message text at the bottom of the reply.

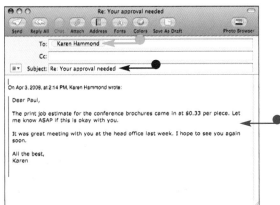

③ Edit the original message to include only the text that is relevant to your reply.

Note: If the original message is fairly short, you usually do not need to edit the text. However, if the original message is long, and your response deals only with part of that message, you will save the recipient time and confusion by deleting everything except the relevant portion of the text.

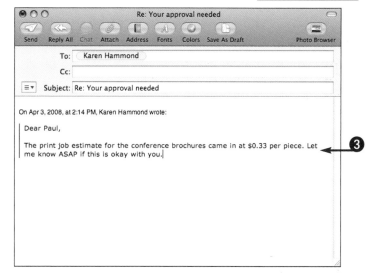

④ Click the area above the original message text and type your reply.

⑤ Click **Send**.

Mail sends your reply.

Note: Mail stores a copy of your reply in the Sent folder.

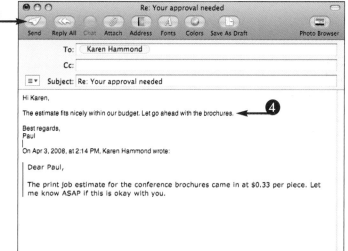

TIPS

I received a message inadvertently. Is there a way that I can pass it along to the correct recipient?

Yes. Mail comes with a feature that enables you to pass along inadvertent messages to the correct recipient. Click the message that you received inadvertently, click **Message,** and then click **Redirect** (or press Shift +⌘+E). Type the recipient's address and then click **Send**. Replies to this message will be sent to the original sender, not to you.

How should I respond to a message that is hostile or rude?

If you receive an unpleasant message, it is best not to respond directly to the sender because that most often just encourages that person to send you more messages. A much better way to handle this situation is to return a *bounce* message that makes it appear your address is not valid. Click the message that you received, click **Message,** and then click **Bounce** (or press Shift+⌘+B).

Forward a Message

If a message has information that is relevant to or concerns another person, you can forward a copy of that message to the other recipient. You can also include your own comments in the forward.

Forward a Message

1 Click the message that you want to forward.

2 Click **Forward**.

Note: You can also press **Shift** + **⌘** + **F**.

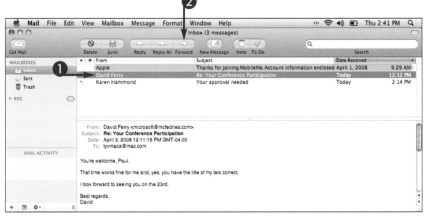

A message window appears.

● Mail inserts the subject line, preceded by Fwd:.

● The original message's addresses (To and From), date, subject, and text are included at the bottom of the forward.

3 Type the e-mail address of the person to whom you are forwarding the message.

4 To send a copy of the forward to another person, type that person's e-mail address (shown here in the Cc line).

⑤ Edit the original message to include only the text that is relevant to your forward.

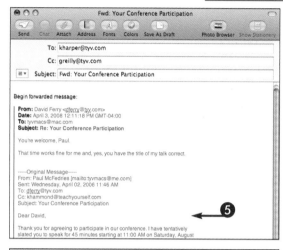

⑥ Click the area above the original message text and type your comments.

⑦ Click **Send**.

Mail sends your forward.

Note: *Mail stores a copy of your forward in the Sent folder.*

Note: *You can forward someone a copy of the actual message instead of just a copy of the message text. Click the message, click* **Message,** *and then click* **Forward As Attachment.** *Mail creates a new message and includes the original message as an attachment.*

TIP

Mail always formats my replies as rich text, even when the original message is plain text. How can I fix this problem?

You can configure Mail to always reply using the same format as the original message. Follow these steps:

① Click **Mail.**

② Click **Preferences.**

The Mail preferences appear.

③ Click the **Composing** tab.

④ Click the **Use the same message format as the original message** check box (changes to ✓).

⑤ Click

Open and Close iChat

Your Mac includes the iChat application to enable you to exchange instant messages with other people who are online. Before you can send or receive instant messages, you must know how to start the iChat application.

The first time you open iChat, you must run through a short configuration process to set up your account.

Open and Close iChat

OPEN ICHAT

1. Click [icon] in the Dock.
2. Click **Applications**.
3. Double-click **iChat**.

CONFIGURE YOUR ICHAT ACCOUNT

The first time you open iChat, the Welcome to iChat dialog box appears.

4. Click **Continue**.

The Account Setup dialog box appears.

⑤ In the Account Type pop-up menu, click and then click the type of account you want to use with iChat.

⑥ Type the account name.

⑦ Type the account password.

⑧ Click **Continue.**

If you are using a MobileMe account, the Encrypted iChat dialog box appears.

⑨ If you do not need to encrypt your messages for security, click **Enable iChat encryption** (☑ changes to ☐).

⑩ Click **Continue.**

The Conclusion dialog box appears.

⑪ Click **Done.**

TIPS

Are there faster methods I can use to open iChat?

The fastest way to start iChat is to click the iChat icon () in the Dock. If you have used iChat recently, another reasonably fast method is to click , click **Recent Items,** and then click **iChat.**

How do I close iChat?

In the menu bar, click **iChat** and then click **Quit iChat.** Probably the fastest method you can use to quit iChat is to Ctrl+click or right-click and then click **Quit.** If your hands are closer to the keyboard than to the mouse, you can quit iChat by pressing ⌘+Q.

You send instant messages to, and receive instant messages from, the people in your *buddy list*, which is also called a *contact list*. Before you can send an instant message to a person, you must add the person to your iChat buddy list.

iChat enables you to maintain your buddy list by adding and deleting people, and it tells you the current online status of each person on the list.

Add a Buddy

❶ Click **Buddies.**

❷ Click **Add Buddy.**

Note: You can also run the Add Buddy command by pressing Shift + ⌘ + A.

iChat prompts you for the buddy's AIM (AOL Instant Messenger) or MobileMe account information.

❸ In the pop-up menu beside the Account Name text box, click 🔽 and then click your buddy's account type: **AIM** or **MobileMe.**

④ Use the Account Name text box to specify your buddy's AIM screen name or MobileMe address.

⑤ Use the First Name text box to type your buddy's first name.

⑥ Use the Last Name text box to type your buddy's last name.

⑦ Click **Add.**

● iChat adds the person to your buddy list.

TIP

Is there a way to change the picture that iChat uses for my buddy?

Yes. By default, iChat uses whatever picture your buddy has configured for himself or herself. To display a different picture, follow these steps:

① Click the buddy.

② Click **Buddies.**

③ Click **Show Info.**

④ Click **Address Card.**

⑤ Click **Always use this picture** (☑ changes to ☐).

⑥ Click and drag the picture you want to use and drop it on the Picture box.

⑦ Click 🖼.

Start a Text Chat

In iChat, an instant-messaging conversation is most often the exchange of text messages between two or more people who are online and available to chat.

An instant-messaging conversation begins by one person inviting another person to exchange messages. In iChat, this means sending an initial instant message, and the recipient either accepts or rejects the invitation.

Start a Text Chat

SEND AN INVITATION

① In iChat's AIM Buddy List, make sure the person's status icon is green (🟢).

Note: The 🟢 icon means that the person is available to chat; a red icon (🔴) means that the person is not available to chat; and a yellow icon (🟡) means the person is idle: available, but not actively using iChat.

② Click the person you want to chat with.

③ Click **Buddies.**

④ Click **Invite to Chat.**

A chat window appears.

⑤ Type your invitation or opening message.

⑥ Press Return.

The invitation appears on the other person's computer.

ACCEPT AN INVITATION

1 Click the invitation.

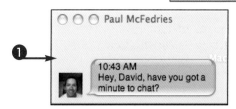

2 Type a response.

Note: *If the person who sent the message is not on your buddy list, iChat does not display the message. To see the message, you must click* **Display.**

3 Click **Accept.**

● If you cannot chat right now, click **Decline,** instead.

● The response appears in the chat window.

4 Repeat Steps **5** and **6** from the previous page to continue chatting.

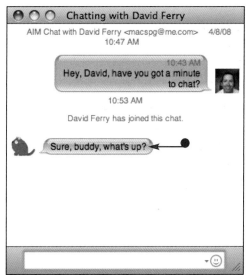

Are there faster methods I can use to start a text chat?

Yes. If your hand is on the mouse, use the AIM Buddy List window to click the person you want to chat with and then click the **Start a Text Chat** button (A). From the keyboard, you can start a text chat with the selected buddy by pressing Shift + ⌘ + M.

Is there a way to automatically decline a person who is bothering me?

Yes, there is. If you no longer want to receive messages from a sender who is annoying, abusive, or offensive, iChat enables you to block that sender. This means that iChat will no longer allow messages from that person to go through. When a chat alert message comes through from that person, click the message and then click **Block.** When iChat asks you to confirm, click **Block** again.

Start an Audio Chat

If you and the buddy with whom you want to converse both have a microphone attached to your computers, a sound card, and speakers, you can converse with each other just as though you were talking over the phone. iChat comes with an *audio chat* feature that enables you to speak to another person over the Internet.

Start an Audio Chat

SEND AN INVITATION

① In iChat's AIM Buddy List, make sure the person's status icon is green (⬤).

Note: *Also make sure that the person shows the telephone icon (📞) or the camera icon (📷), which means the person has the equipment required for an audio chat.*

② Click the person you want to audio chat with.

③ Click **Buddies.**

④ Click **Invite to Audio Chat.**

An audio chat window appears and iChat waits for a response to the invitation.

The invitation appears on the other person's computer.

ACCEPT AN INVITATION

1 Click the invitation.

2 Click **Accept.**

● If you prefer to text chat, click **Text Reply** to begin a separate text chat.

● If you cannot chat right now, click **Decline.**

iChat sets up the audio connection.

3 Use your microphone to converse with the other person.

● You can click and drag the slider to control the chat volume.

TIPS

Can I start a video chat?
Yes, if you and the contact with whom you want to converse both have a Web camera, microphone, sound card, and speakers attached to your computer, you can both see and talk to each other at the same time. iChat comes with a *video chat* feature that enables you to see each other's Web camera image and hear each other's voice. If the other person shows the camera icon (📷), click that person, click **Buddies,** and then click **Invite to Video Chat.**

Are there faster methods I can use to start an audio or video chat?
Yes. First, use the AIM Buddy List window to click the person you want to chat with. For an audio chat, click the **Start an Audio Chat** button (📞); for a video chat, click the **Start a Video Chat** button (📹).

CHAPTER

10

Working with Contacts and Appointments

You may find that your life is busier than ever, and the number of appointments you have to keep and tasks you have to perform seem to increase daily. Fortunately, your Mac comes with two applications that can help you manage your busy schedule. You use Address Book to manage your contacts, and you use iCal to enter and track appointments and to-do items.

Open and Close Address Book

Your Mac includes the Address Book application to enable you to manage your contacts, whether they are colleagues, friends, or family members. Before you can add or work with contacts, you must know how to start the Address Book application.

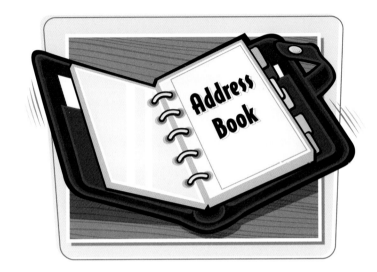

Open and Close Address Book

OPEN ADDRESS BOOK

1. Click the **Finder icon** (🖥️) in the Dock.

2. Click **Applications.**

3. Double-click **Address Book.**

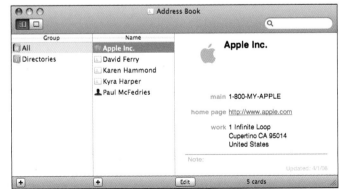

The Address Book window appears.

CLOSE ADDRESS BOOK

1 Click **Address Book.**

2 Click **Quit Address Book.**

TIPS

Are there faster methods I can use to open Address Book?

The fastest way to start Address Book is to click the Address Book icon (📖) in the Dock. If you have used Address Book recently, another reasonably fast method is to click ➗, click **Recent Items,** and then click **Address Book.**

Are there faster methods I can use to close Address Book?

Probably the fastest method you can use to quit Address Book is to Ctrl +click or right-click 📖 and then click **Quit.** If your hands are closer to the keyboard than to the mouse, you can quit Address Book by pressing ⌘+Q.

Add a New Contact

You can store contact information for a particular person by creating a card for that person in Address Book. You can store a person's name, company name, phone numbers, address, and much more.

Add a New Contact

1 Click **File**.

2 Click **New Card**.

Note: You can also run the New Card command by pressing ⌘+N or by clicking ⊞ in the Name column.

● Address Book adds a new card.

3 Use the First field to type the contact's first name.

4 Use the Last field to type the contact's last name.

5 Use the Company field to type the contact's company name.

6 If the contact is a company, click **Company** (☐ changes to ☑).

chapter **10**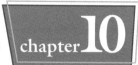

⑦ In the first Phone field, click ⊟ and then click the category you want to use.

⑧ Type the phone number.

⑨ Repeat Steps **7** and **8** to enter data in some or all of the other fields.

Note: *See the next section to learn how to add more fields to the card.*

⑩ Click **Edit.**

Address Book saves the new card.

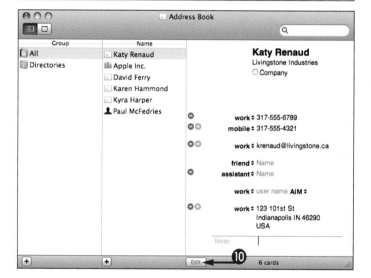

If I include a contact's e-mail address, is there a way to send that person a message without having to type the address?

Yes. You can follow these steps:

① Click the contact's card.

② Click the e-mail address category.

③ Click **Send Email.**

Apple Mail displays a new e-mail message with the contact already added in the To line.

④ Fill in the rest of the message as required.

⑤ Click **Send.**

Note, too, that you can also start a new message in Mail: click **Address,** click the contact, and then click **To:** (or **Cc:** or **Bcc:**).

Edit a Contact

If you need to make changes to the information already in a contact's card, or if you need to add new information to a card, you can edit the card from within Address Book.

Edit a Contact

1 Click the card you want to edit.

2 Click **Edit.**

● Address Book makes the card's fields available for editing.

3 Edit the existing fields as required.

4 To add a field, click 🔘.

Note: *Address Book adds a field of the same type. For example, if you click 🔘 in the Phone area, Address Book adds a new Phone field.*

5 To remove a field, click 🔘.

⑥ To add a new field type, click **Card.**

⑦ Click **Add Field.**

⑧ Click the type of field you want.

● Address Book adds the field to the card.

⑨ When you are done, click **Edit.**

Address Book saves the edited card.

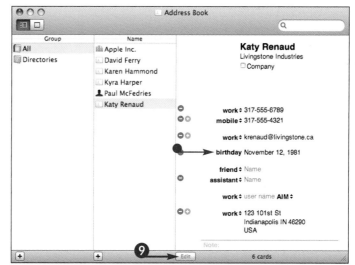

TIP

How do I add a picture for the new contact?
Follow these steps:

① Click the contact's card.

② Click **Edit** and double-click the picture box.

③ Click **Choose** and choose the picture you want to use.

④ Click **Open.**

⑤ Click and drag the picture to the position you want.

⑥ Click **Set.**

⑦ Click **Edit.**

Create a Contact Group

You can organize your contacts into one or more groups, which is useful if you want to view just a subset of your contacts. You can create a group first and then add members, or you can select members in advance and then create the group.

CREATE A CONTACT GROUP

① Click **File.**

② Click **New Group.**

Note: You can also run the New Group command by pressing **Shift** + **⌘** + **N** *or by clicking in the Group column.*

● Address Book adds a new group.

③ Type a name for the group.

④ Press **Return**.

⑤ Click **All.**

⑥ Click and drag a contact to the group.

Address Book adds the contact to the group.

⑦ Repeat Step **6** for the other contacts you want to add to the group.

CREATE A GROUP OF SELECTED CONTACTS

① Select the contacts you want to include in the new group.

Note: To select multiple contacts, press and hold ⌘ *and click each card.*

② Click **File.**

③ Click **New Group From Selection.**

● Address Book adds a new group.

● Address Book adds the selected contacts as group members.

④ Type a name for the group.

⑤ Press Return.

 TIPS

Can I send an e-mail message to the group?

Yes, this is one of the best reasons to create a group. Normally, sending an e-mail message to multiple contacts involves typing or selecting multiple addresses. With a group, however, you send a single message to the group, and Mail automatically sends a copy to each member. Ctrl+click or right-click the group and then click **Send Email to "*Group*",** where *Group* is the name of the group.

What is a smart group?

A smart group is a special group where each member has one or more fields in common, such as the company name, department name, city, or state. When you create the smart group, you specify one or more criteria, and then Address Book automatically adds members to the group if they meet those criteria. To create a smart group, click **File,** click **New Smart Group,** and then enter your group criteria.

Open and Close iCal

Your Mac includes the iCal application to enable you to manage your schedule. Before you can add or work with events (appointments and all-day activities), and to-do items (tasks), you must know how to start the iCal application.

OPEN ICAL

1 Click in the Dock.

2 Click **Applications**.

3 Double-click **iCal**.

The iCal window appears.

CLOSE ICAL

① Click **iCal.**

② Click **Quit iCal.**

TIPS

Are there faster methods I can use to open iCal?

The fastest way to start iCal is to click the iCal icon (🔟) in the Dock. If you have used iCal recently, another reasonably fast method is to click 🍎, click **Recent Items,** and then click **iCal.**

Are there faster methods I can use to close iCal?

Probably the fastest method you can use to quit iCal is to Ctrl+click or right-click 🔟 and then click **Quit.** If your hands are closer to the keyboard than to the mouse, you can quit iCal by pressing ⌘+Q.

Before you create an
appointment or all-day event,
you must first select the date on
which the appointment or event
occurs.

Navigate the Calendar

USE THE MINI-MONTH

1 In the mini-month, click the **Next
Month** button (▶) until the
month of your appointment
appears.

● If you go too far, click the
Previous Month button (◀) to
move back to the month you
want.

2 Click the date.

● The date appears in the
appointments list.

● To see just that date, click **Day**
(or press ⌘+①).

● To see the date in the context of
its month, click **Month** (or
press ⌘+③).

● If you want to return to today's
date, click **Today** (or press
⌘+Ⓣ).

GO TO A SPECIFIC DATE

1 Click **View.**

2 Click **Go to Date.**

You can also select the Go to Date command by pressing Shift + ⌘ + T.

The Go to date dialog box appears.

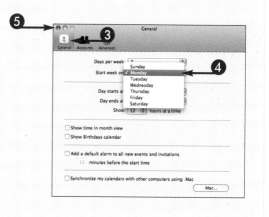

3 Use the Date text box to type the date you want using the format mm/dd/yyyy.

● You can also click the day, month, or year and then click ⁞ to increase or decrease the value.

4 Click **Show.**

iCal displays the date in the appointments list.

In the Week view, the week begins on Sunday. How can I change this to Monday?

iCal's default Week view has Sunday on the left and Saturday on the right. Many people prefer to display the weekend days together, with Monday on the left signaling the start of the week. To set this up, follow these steps:

1 Click **iCal** in the menu bar.

2 Click **Preferences.**

3 Click the **General** tab.

4 In the Start week on pop-up menu, click ⁞ and then click **Monday.**

5 Click 🔘.

Create an Appointment

You can help organize your life by using iCal to record your appointments — which iCal calls *events* — on the date and time they occur.

If the event has no set time – for example, a birthday, anniversary, or multiple-day event such as a sales meeting or vacation – you can create an all-day appointment.

Create an Appointment

CREATE A REGULAR APPOINTMENT

1. Navigate to the date when the appointment occurs.

2. Click the calendar you want to use.

3. Double-click the time when the appointment starts.

● iCal adds a one-hour appointment.

Note: *If the appointment is less than or more than an hour, you can also click and drag the mouse (↖) over the full appointment period.*

4. Type the name of the event.

5. Press Return.

Note: *Another way to create a new appointment is to click the start time and then press ⌘ + N.*

CREATE AN ALL-DAY APPOINTMENT

1 Navigate to the date when the appointment occurs.

2 Click the calendar you want to use.

3 Double-click anywhere inside the all-day section.

● iCal adds a new all-day appointment.

4 Type the name of the event.

5 Press Return.

TIP

How can I specify event details such as the location and a reminder message?

Follow these steps:

1 Follow the steps in this section to create an appointment.

2 Double-click the appointment.

If this is the first time you have edited the appointment, skip to Step **4**.

3 Click **Edit**.

4 Use the location text box to type the location of the event.

5 Use the alarm pop-up menu to choose **Message.**

6 Choose the amount of time before the appointment that you want to receive the reminder.

7 Click **Done.**

iCal saves the new appointment configuration.

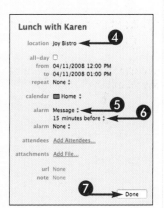

Create a Repeating Appointment

If you have an activity or appointment that recurs at a regular interval, you can create an event and configure it to automatically repeat in iCal. You can repeat an event daily, weekly, monthly, yearly, or with a custom interval.

Create a Repeating Appointment

① Follow the steps in the previous section to create an appointment.

② Double-click the appointment.

iCal displays information for the event.

Note: *You do not see this information the first time you double-click an appointment, in which case you can skip to Step 4.*

③ Click **Edit**.

iCal opens the appointment for editing.

④ Beside the repeat label, click **None.**

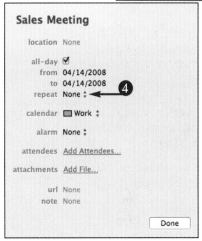

⑤ Click the interval you want to use.

● If you want to specify a custom interval such as every two weeks or the first Monday of every month, click **Custom** and configure your interval in the dialog box that appears.

⑥ Click **Done.**

iCal adds the repeating appointments to the calendar.

TIPS

How do I configure an event to stop after a certain number of occurrences?
Follow these steps:

① Follow Steps **1** to **5** to select a recurrence interval.

② Beside the end label, click **None** and then click **After.**

③ Type the number of occurrences you want.

④ Click **Done.**

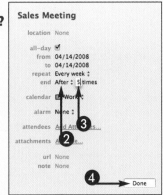

Is it possible to delete just a single occurrence out of a recurring series of events?

Yes, you can delete one occurrence from the calendar without affecting the rest of the series. Click the occurrence you want to delete, and then press Del. iCal asks whether you want to delete all the occurrences or just the selected occurrence. Click **Delete Only This Event.**

Create a To-Do Item

You can monitor to-do items — from large projects such as budgets to basic chores such as returning phone calls — by using iCal to record these tasks. You can help organize your life by giving a priority to each task.

When the to-do item is done, you should mark it as complete so you can easily tell which items remain to be done.

Create a To-Do Item

CREATE A TO-DO ITEM

① Click the calendar you want to use.

② Click **File**.

③ Click **New To Do**.

Note: You can also choose the New To Do command by pressing ⌘+K.

● iCal displays the To Do list.

● iCal adds a new to-do item to the list.

● You can click **View or Hide To Dos** (⊠) to toggle the To Do list on and off.

④ Type the name of the to-do item.

⑤ Press Return.

SET THE PRIORITY

1 Click the **Set Priority** icon (☰).

2 Click the priority you want to use.

MARK A TO DO ITEM AS COMPLETED

1 Click the **Completed** check box (☐ changes to ☑).

How can I specify to-do item details such as the due date and a reminder message?

Follow these steps:

1 Follow the steps in this section to create a to-do item.

2 In the To Do list, double-click the to-do item.

3 Click **due date** (☐ changes to ☑).

4 Type the date the to-do item is due.

5 Use the alarm pop-up menu to choose **Message.**

6 Choose when you want to receive the reminder.

7 Type the time you want the reminder to appear.

8 Click **Done.**

iCal saves the new to-do item configuration.

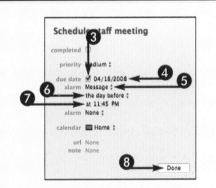

CHAPTER

11

Working with Your MobileMe Account

For an annual fee, you can get a MobileMe account, which is a Web-based service that gives you e-mail, an address book, a calendar, a Web Gallery for sharing photos, and online file storage. This chapter shows you how to use all of these features of MobileMe.

Log in to MobileMe

Before you can use any of the features associated with your MobileMe account, you must log in to the service.

Log in to MobileMe

① In your Web browser, type **http://www.me.com/**.

② Press Return.

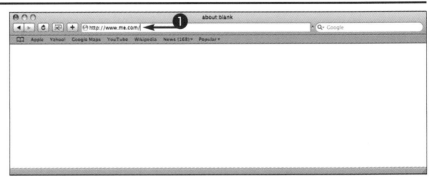

The MobileMe Login page appears.

③ Use the Member name text box to type your MobileMe ID, which is your member name followed by @me.com.

④ Use the Password text box to type the password for your MobileMe account.

- If you want MobileMe to log you in automatically for two weeks, click **Keep me logged in for two weeks** (☐ changes to ☑).

5️⃣ Click **Log In**.

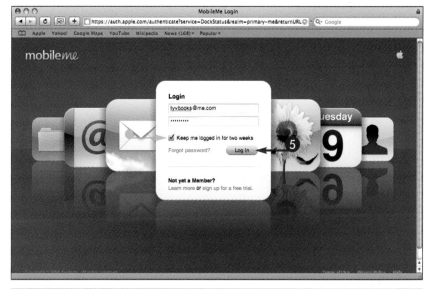

Your main MobileMe account page appears.

- When you are done working with your MobileMe account, click **Log Out** to log out of the account.

TIPS

How do I get a MobileMe account?
Follow Steps **1** and **2**, click **sign up for a free trial**, and then fill in the form. You will be able to try out MobileMe free for 60 days, and then to continue you must pay a subscription fee. A Basic Membership currently costs $99 per year; a Family Pack membership currently costs $149 per year and consists of one main account plus four subaccounts.

Can I log in from my Mac?
Yes. Click the **System Preferences Icon** (🖼️) in the Dock (or click 🍎 and then click **System Preferences**) and then click **MobileMe**. (If you see .Mac instead, click 🍎, click **Software Update,** and then install the **Mac OS X Update for MobileMe**.) Type your member name and password, and then click **Sign In**.

Are you a MobileMe member?
Sign into your account to set up MobileMe on this computer.

Member Name: tyvbooks

Password: •••••••••

(Sign In)

Send and Receive MobileMe Mail

You can use the MobileMe Mail feature to work with your MobileMe e-mail account online. You can check for incoming messages, reply to messages, or send new messages, using either your Mac or any computer with Web access.

DISPLAY MOBILEME MAIL

① Log in to your MobileMe account.

Note: See the "Log in to MobileMe" section, earlier in this chapter.

② Click **Mail.**

GET INCOMING MESSAGES

① Click **Get Mail.**

MobileMe Mail checks for incoming messages and, if there are any, it displays them in the Inbox folder.

REPLY TO A MESSAGE

① Click the message.

② Click **Reply to sender.**

● To reply to all the recipients of the original message, click **Reply to all recipients** instead.

● To pass the message to another person, click **Forward** instead.

③ In the message window that appears (not shown), type your message and then click **Send message.**

SEND A NEW MESSAGE

① Click **Compose new message**.

The New Message window appears.

② Use the To text box to type the recipient's e-mail address.

● If you want another person to see a copy of the message, type that person's address in the Cc text box.

③ Use the Subject text box to type the subject of the message.

④ Type your message.

⑤ Click **Send message.**

I am receiving spam on my MobileMe e-mail account. Can MobileMe Mail block these messages?

Yes, MobileMe Mail comes with a junk-mail filter feature that marks spam messages as junk and optionally moves those messages to the Junk folder. To activate this feature, open MobileMe Mail, click ![icon], click **Preferences,** and then click the **General** tab. Click **Enable junk mail filtering** (☐ changes to ☑). To use the Junk folder, also click the **Automatically move messages marked as junk to the Junk folder** check box (☐ changes to ☑). Click **Save.**

Can I use MobileMe Mail to check e-mail from another account?

Yes, MobileMe Mail allows you to check incoming mail on one POP (Post Office Protocol) account, such as your ISP account. Open MobileMe Mail, click ![icon], click **Preferences,** and then click the **Other** tab. Click **Check mail from an external POP account** (☐ changes to ☑), and then fill in your e-mail address, User name, Password, and Incoming mail server address. Click **Save.**

Work with MobileMe Contacts

You can use MobileMe to store information about your friends, family, colleagues, and clients. Using the Contacts application, you can store data such as the person's name, phone numbers, e-mail address, and street address.

If you already have contacts in your Mac Address Book, you can synchronize them with MobileMe. See "Synchronize Your Mac with MobileMe," later in this chapter.

Work with MobileMe Contacts

DISPLAY MOBILEME CONTACTS

1 Log in to your MobileMe account.

Note: See the "Log in to MobileMe" section, earlier in this chapter.

2 Click **Contacts.**

CREATE A CONTACT

1 Click **Create a new contact.**

2 Type the person's first name.

3 Type the person's last name.

4 Type the person company name.

5 Click here and then click a phone number category.

6 Type the phone number.

7 Click here and then click an e-mail category.

8 Type the person's e-mail address.

9 Click here and then click a street address category.

10 Use the text boxes in this section to type the person's street address.

11 Type a note about the person.

12 Click **Save.**

MobileMe saves the contact.

DISPLAY A CONTACT

1 Use the scroll bar to locate the contact.

2 Click the contact.

● MobileMe displays the contact's details.

● You can also type part of the contact's name in the Search box.

● To e-mail the contact, click the e-mail address.

● To make changes to the contact, click **Edit.**

● To remove the contact, click **Delete.**

How do I add a photo for a contact?

To add a photo to an existing contact, click the contact and then click **Edit.** Click **Add** to open the Add Photo dialog box, click **Choose Photo,** click the photo you want to use, click **Choose,** and then click **OK.** Note that you can only use GIF, JPEG, or PNG files that are no larger than 1MB.

Is there any way to store data such as the person's birthday or job title?

Yes, the Contacts application offers a number of other fields, including Birthday, Job Title, Nickname, Prefix, and Suffix. To add a field to an existing contact, click the contact and then click **Edit.** Click Add Field, click the field you want, and then edit the field data. Note, too, that you can also add more instances of some fields by clicking the green + icon to the right of a field.

Manage Your Schedule with MobileMe

You can use MobileMe to manage your schedule. Using the Calendar application, you can add events (appointments and all-day activities) and to-do items (tasks).

If you already have appointments in your Mac iCal application, you can synchronize them with MobileMe. See "Synchronize Your Mac with MobileMe," later in this chapter.

Manage Your Schedule with MobileMe

DISPLAY MOBILEME CALENDAR

① Log in to your MobileMe account.

Note: *See the "Log in to MobileMe" section, earlier in this chapter.*

② Click **Calendar.**

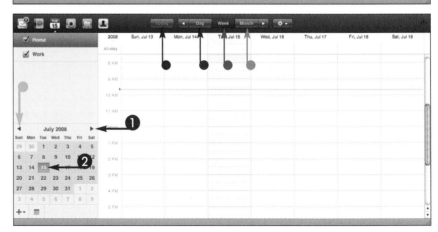

NAVIGATE CALENDAR

① Click **Next Month** (▶) until the month you want appears.

● Click **Previous Month** (◀) to move back to the month you want.

② Click the date.

● To see just that date, click **Day.**

● To see the date in the context of its week, click **Week.**

● To see the date in the context of its month, click **Month.**

● To return to today's date, click **Today.**

CREATE AN EVENT

1 Navigate to the date when the appointment occurs.

2 Click the calendar you want to use.

3 Double-click the time when the event starts.

● Calendar adds a one-hour event.

Note: *If the event is less than or more than an hour, you can also click and drag the mouse (⟍) over the full appointment period.*

4 Type the name of the event.

5 Press **Return**.

EDIT AN EVENT

1 Double-click the event.

2 Edit the event details as needed.

● If the event lasts all day, click **All-Day Event** (☐ changes to ☑).

3 Click **OK.**

 TIPS

How do I create a to-do item?

Click ⚙▾ and then click **New To Do.** MobileMe displays the To Dos by Priority list and adds a new to-do item. Type the to-do item text and then press **Return**. To change the priority, click the **Priority** button in the right of the to-do item and the click **None, Low, Medium,** or **High.**

How do I change the time zone?

Click ⚙▾ and the click **Preferences** to open the Calendar Preferences. Click the Advanced tab and then click **Turn on time zone support** (☐ changes to ☑). Click the **Time zone** menu and then click the time zone you want to use. Click **Save.** MobileMe reloads and displays the new time zone in the browser's title bar.

Share Photos with MobileMe

You can use MobileMe to upload photos and share them with others. Using the Gallery application, you can create different photo albums and make those albums available for others to see.

You can also configure a photo album to allow others to upload and download photos.

CREATE A PHOTO ALBUM

① Log in to your MobileMe account.

Note: See the "Log in to MobileMe" section, earlier in this chapter.

② Click **Gallery.**

③ Click **Create a New Album.**

④ Type the album name.

⑤ To allow Web uploading, click **Uploading of photos via web browser** (☐ changes to ☑).

⑥ To allow e-mail uploading, click **Adding of photos via email or iPhone** (☐ changes to ☑).

⑦ To allow downloading, click **Downloading of photos or entire album** (☐ changes to ☑).

⑧ Click **Create.**

UPLOAD PHOTOS

1 Click the album.

2 Click **Upload.**

The Uploads window appears.

3 Click **Close this window when complete** (☐ changes to ☑).

4 Click **Choose.**

5 Select the photos you want to upload.

6 Click **Select.**

MobileMe uploads the photos to the album.

TIPS

Can I upload photos to an album using my iPhone?

Sure, as long as you're using the iPhone 2.0 software. On your iPhone's Home screen, tap Photos, tap the photo album that contains the photo you want to upload, tap the photo, tap the Action icon in the lower-left corner, and then tap Send to MobileMe. Tap the album you want to use for the photo. In the new e-mail message, type a photo title in the Subject field and then tap Send.

How do people view my MobileMe Gallery?

People can view your MobileMe Gallery using any Web browser. The address of your gallery is shown in the upper-right corner of the Gallery application. The format is http://gallery.me.com/*Username*, where *Username* is your MobileMe username.

Upload Files to Your iDisk

You can store files with your MobileMe account by using the iDisk online storage feature. With iDisk, you upload files from your Mac and store them in iDisk folders such as Pictures, Documents, and Backup.

You can use iDisk to make backup copies of important documents. Because you can access your iDisk from any computer over the Web, you can also use iDisk to make certain files available to you from anywhere that has Internet access.

Upload Files to Your iDisk

DISPLAY MOBILEME IDISK

1 Log in to your MobileMe account.

Note: *See the "Log in to MobileMe" section, earlier in this chapter.*

2 Click **iDisk**.

UPLOAD A FILE USING MOBILEME

1 Click the folder you want to use to store the file.

2 Click **Upload**.

The Uploads window appears.

3 Click **Close this window when complete** (☐ changes to ☑).

4 Click **Choose**.

⑤ Select the file you want to upload.

⑥ Click **Select.**

MobileMe uploads the file to your iDisk.

UPLOAD A FILE USING YOUR MAC

① Click the **Finder icon** ().

② Click **iDisk.**

③ Click the folder to which you want to upload the file.

④ Press ⌘+N.

A new Finder window appears.

⑤ Open the folder that contains the file you want to upload.

⑥ Click and drag the file and drop it inside the iDisk folder.

Your Mac uploads the file to your iDisk.

You can now access your uploaded files online.

TIPS

Can I access my iDisk from Windows?

Yes, if you also have a Windows computer at home or at work, you can use it to access your iDisk. Open a Web browser and enter the address **http://idisk.mac.com/username/**, where *username* is your MobileMe member name. When Windows asks you to log on, type your MobileMe member name and password, and then click **OK.**

Can I use iDisk to share files with other people over the Web?

Yes, you can use the Public folder to do this. Other people can then use a Web browser to enter the address **http://public.me.com/username/**, where *username* is your MobileMe member name. No password is required, so others can easily work with these files. Because the Public folder does not require a password, do not use it to store files that contain confidential or sensitive data.

Synchronize Your Mac with MobileMe

You can ensure that your Mac and your MobileMe account have the same data by synchronizing the two. You can synchronize bookmarks, iCal appointments, Address Book contacts, e-mail accounts, and more.

If you have a second Mac, you can also synchronize it with the same MobileMe account, which ensures that your two Macs use the same data.

Synchronize Your Mac with MobileMe

① Log in to your MobileMe account.

Note: See the "Log in to MobileMe" section, earlier in this chapter.

② Click the **Apple Icon** (🍎).

③ Click **System Preferences.**

Note: You can also open System Preferences by clicking 📷 on the Dock.

The System Preferences window appears.

④ Click **MobileMe.**

The MobileMe preferences appear.

❺ Click **Sync.**

❻ Click **Synchronize with MobileMe** (☐ changes to ☑).

● Your Mac registers itself with your MobileMe account.

❼ Click the check box beside each type of data you want to synchronize (☐ changes to ☑).

❽ Click **Sync Now.**

Your Mac synchronizes the data with your MobileMe account.

TIPS

Is there a way to have my Mac synchronize with my MobileMe account on a schedule?

Yes, you can configure your MobileMe preferences to perform an automatic synchronization at regular intervals. Follow Steps **1** to **6** to enable the synchronization. In the **Synchronize with MobileMe** list, click and then click the interval you want: **Every Hour, Every Day,** or **Every Week.**

What happens if I modify an appointment, contact, bookmark, or other data in MobileMe?

The synchronization process works both ways. That is, all the Mac data you selected to synchronize is sent to your MobileMe account. However, the data on your MobileMe account is also sent to your Mac. This means that if you modify, add, or delete data on your MobileMe account, those changes are also reflected in your Mac data.

CHAPTER 12

Customizing Your Mac

Your Mac comes with a number of features that enable you to customize your computer. Not only can you change the appearance of your Mac to suit your taste, but you can also change the way your Mac works to make it easier to use and more efficient.

Display System Preferences

You can find many of your Mac's customization features in System Preferences, a collection of settings and options that control the overall look and operation of your Mac. To use these settings, you must know how to display the System Preferences window.

OPEN SYSTEM PREFERENCES

1 Click the **Apple Icon** (🍎).

2 Click **System Preferences**.

The **System Preferences** window appears.

CLOSE SYSTEM PREFERENCES

① Click **System Preferences.**

② Click **Quit System Preferences.**

TIPS

Are there faster methods I can use to open and close System Preferences?

The fastest way to start **System Preferences** is to click the **System Preferences** icon (🔲) in the Dock. Probably the fastest method you can use to quit **System Preferences** is to click 🔲. Alternatively, Ctrl+click or right-click 🔲 and then click **Quit.** Finally, if your hands are closer to the keyboard than to the mouse, you can quit System Preferences by pressing ⌘+Q.

Sometimes when I open System Preferences I do not see all the icons. How can I restore the original icons?

When you click an icon in System Preferences, the window changes to show just the options and settings associated with that icon. To return to the main System Preferences window, you have two choices:

● Click ◄ until the main window appears.

● Click **Show All.**

Change the Desktop Background

To give your Mac a different look, you can change the desktop background to display either a different image or a solid color.

You can change the desktop background to show either a fixed image or a series of images that change periodically.

SET A FIXED BACKGROUND IMAGE

① Open System Preferences.

Note: See the "Display System Preferences" section, earlier in this chapter.

② Click **Desktop & Screen Saver.**

The desktop and screen saver preferences appear.

③ Click **Desktop.**

④ Click the image category you want to use.

⑤ Click the image you want to use as the desktop background.

Your Mac changes the desktop background.

⑥ If you chose a photo in Step **5,** click ⬌ and then click an item to determine how your Mac displays the photo.

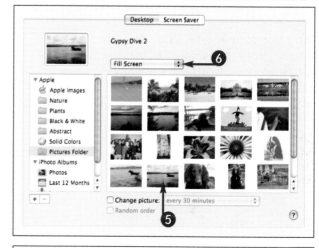

SET A CHANGING BACKGROUND IMAGE

① Click **Change picture** (☐ changes to ☑).

② Click ⬌ in the list and then click how often you want the background image to change.

③ If you want your Mac to choose the periodic image randomly, click **Random order** (☐ changes to ☑).

Your Mac changes the desktop background periodically based on your chosen interval.

When I choose a photo, what is the difference between the various options for displaying the photo?

Your Mac gives you five options for displaying the photo:

Fit to Screen This option expands the photo in all four directions until the photo is either the same height as the desktop or the same width as the desktop.

Fill Screen This option expands the photo by the same amount in all four directions until it fills the entire desktop. This option can cause some edges of the photo to be cropped out.

Stretch to Fill Screen This option expands the photo in all four directions until it fills the entire desktop. Because the photo is usually expanded more either vertically or horizontally, this option can cause the photo to appear distorted.

Tile This option repeats your photo multiple times to fill the entire desktop.

Center This option displays the photo at its actual size and places the photo in the center of the desktop.

Activate the Screen Saver

You can set up your Mac to display a *screen saver,* a moving pattern or series of pictures. The screen saver appears after your computer has been idle for a while.

If you leave your monitor on for long stretches while your computer is idle, a faint version of the unmoving image can endure for awhile on the screen, a phenomenon known as *persistence.* A screen saver prevents this by displaying a moving image.

Activate the Screen Saver

1 Open System Preferences.

Note: See the "Display System Preferences" section, earlier in this chapter.

2 Click **Desktop & Screen Saver.**

The desktop and screen saver preferences appear.

3 Click **Screen Saver.**

4 Click the screen saver you want to use.

- A preview of the screen saver appears here.

5 Click and drag the **Start screen saver** slider () to set when the screen saver begins.

Note: The interval you choose is the number of minutes or hours that your Mac must be idle before the screen saver starts.

- If the screen saver is customizable, click **Options** to configure it.

- If you also want to see the current time when the screen saver is active, click **Show with clock** (☐ changes to ☑).

- If you want to see a different screen saver each time, click **Use random screen saver** (☐ changes to ☑).

TIP

What are hot corners and how do I configure them?

A *hot corner* is a corner of your Mac's screen that you have set up to perform some action when you move the mouse (▸) to that corner. To configure hot corners, follow these steps:

1 Follow Steps **1** to **4** to select a screen saver.

2 Click **Hot Corners.**

System Preferences displays the Active Screen Corners dialog box.

3 In the top-left pop-up menu, click ▴ and then click the action you want to perform when you move ▸ to the top-left corner of the screen.

4 Click ▴ and then click the action you want to perform when you move ▸ to the top-right corner of the screen.

5 Click ▴ and then click the action you want to perform when you move ▸ to the bottom-left corner of the screen.

6 Click ▴ and then click the action you want to perform when you move ▸ to the bottom-right corner of the screen.

7 Click **OK.**

Set Your Mac's Sleep Options

You can make your Mac more energy efficient by putting the display or the entire computer to sleep after a period of inactivity.

Sleep mode means that your display or your Mac is in a temporary low-power mode. This saves energy on all Macs, and also saves battery power on a notebook Mac.

Set Your Mac's Sleep Options

1 Open System Preferences.

Note: *See the "Display System Preferences" section, earlier in this chapter.*

2 Click **Energy Saver.**

The Energy Saver preferences appear.

3 With a notebook Mac, use the **Settings for** pop-up menu to click ↕ and then click either **Power Adapter** or **Battery.**

4 With a notebook Mac, use the **Optimization** pop-up menu to click ↕ and then click one of the energy settings.

⑤ If you want to specify custom settings, click **Show Details.**

The Energy Saver preferences window expands to show the sleep settings.

⑥ Click **Sleep.**

⑦ Click and drag 🔘 to set the computer sleep timer.

This specifies the period of inactivity after which your computer goes to sleep.

⑧ Click and drag 🔘 to set the display sleep timer.

This specifies the period of inactivity after which your display goes to sleep.

How do I wake up a sleeping display or computer?

If your Mac's display is in sleep mode, you can wake up the display either by moving your mouse or by pressing any key on your keyboard. If your entire Mac is in sleep mode, you wake up the computer either by clicking the mouse or by pressing any key on your keyboard.

What is the difference between the various energy settings in the Optimization pop-up menu?

Saving energy with a computer is always a tradeoff: the more energy you save, the poorer the computer's performance (because you must wait for devices to wake up). The Better Energy Savings and Better Battery Life items put the display and computer to sleep faster than the Better Performance item. The Normal item uses settings in between these two extremes.

Change the Display Resolution

You can change the resolution of your Mac's display. This enables you to adjust the display for best viewing or for maximum compatibility with whatever application you are using.

You can change your Mac's display resolution using either the System Preferences window or the menu bar.

Change the Display Resolution

CHANGE RESOLUTION VIA THE DISPLAY PREFERENCES

① Open System Preferences.

Note: *See the "Display System Preferences" section, earlier in this chapter.*

② Click **Displays.**

The displays preferences appear.

③ Click **Display.**

④ Click the resolution you want to use.

Your Mac adjusts the screen to the new resolution.

● To change the resolution using your Mac's menu bar, as described on the next page, click **Show displays in menu bar** (☐ changes to ☑).

CHANGE RESOLUTION VIA THE MENU BAR

1 Click the Displays icon (🖥).

Your Mac opens a menu that shows the three most-recently used resolutions.

● The resolution with the check mark (✓) is the current resolution.

2 Click the resolution you want to use.

Your Mac adjusts the screen to the new resolution.

 TIPS

What do the resolution numbers mean?

The resolution numbers are expressed in *pixels*, short for picture elements, which are the individual dots that make up what you see on your Mac's screen. The pixels are arranged in rows and columns, and the resolution tells you the number of pixels that are in each row and column. So a resolution of 1024 x 768 means that the display is using 1,024-pixel rows and 768-pixel columns.

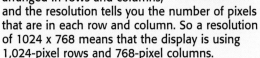

Why do some resolutions also include the word "stretched"?

Most older displays are made with the ratio of the width to the height — this is called the *aspect ratio* — set at 4:3. However, most new Mac displays are made with an aspect ratio of 16:10, which is called *widescreen*. Resolutions designed for 4:3 displays — such as 800 x 600 and 1024 x 768 — take up only part of a widescreen display. To make them take up the entire display, choose the *stretched* version of the resolution.

Change Your Mac's Name

You can give your Mac a distinctive or easier name. By default, your Mac's computer name is your name followed by *'s Mac* — for example, Karen Hammond's Mac.

You can also change your Mac's network name, which is the computer name with spaces replaced with hyphens (-), other symbols removed, and .*local* added — for example, Karen-Hammonds-Mac.local.

CHANGE YOUR MAC'S COMPUTER NAME

❶ Open System Preferences.

Note: *See the "Display System Preferences" section, earlier in this chapter.*

❷ Click **Sharing**.

The Sharing preferences appear.

❸ Use the Computer Name text box to type the name you want to use.

❹ Press Return.

Your Mac sets the new computer name.

**CHANGE YOUR MAC'S
NETWORK NAME**

5 Click **Edit.**

6 Use the Local Hostname text box to type the network name you want to use.

Note: You cannot edit the .local part of the network name.

7 Click **OK.**

Your Mac sets the new network name.

TIPS

Are there any restrictions on the computer name or network name?

Yes. The computer name must be 63 characters or less and can include any character except at (@), equals (=), and colon (:). The network name must be 63 characters or less and it can use only letters, numbers, and hyphens (-).

Why should I change my Mac's computer or network name?

If you activate file sharing as described in Chapter 13, your Mac's computer name appears in the Finder's sidebar and in the Network folder. A different name might make it easier for other people to access or find your Mac on your network.

Other people can use the network name to connect to your Mac manually, so a shorter name makes this easier.

Customize the Dock

You can make the Dock take up less room on the screen, or you can make the Dock easier to access and use, by modifying a few Dock preferences.

① Open System Preferences.

Note: See the "Display System Preferences" section, earlier in this chapter.

② Click **Dock.**

The Dock preferences appear.

③ Click and drag the **Size** to make the Dock smaller or larger.

● System Preferences adjusts the size of the Dock.

Note: If your Dock is already as wide as the screen, dragging the Size slider to the right (toward the Large value) will not have any effect.

④ Click **Magnification** (☐ changes to ☑).

⑤ Click and drag the **Magnification slider** (⬭) to set the magnification level.

● When you position the mouse (▶) over a Dock icon, your Mac magnifies the icon.

⑥ Use the **Position on screen** options to click where you want the Dock to appear, such as the **Left** side of the screen (○ changes to ⦿).

● Your Mac moves the Dock to the new position.

⑦ In the Minimize using pop-up menu, click 🔹 and then click the effect you want your Mac to use when you minimize a window: **Genie Effect** or **Scale Effect**.

TIP

Are there easier methods I can use to control some of these preferences?
Yes, your Mac gives you an easier way to turn Dock magnification on and off and to change the Dock position. Click the **Apple Icon** (🍎) and then click **Dock.** Click **Turn Magnification On** to enable the magnification feature; click **Turn Magnification Off** to disable this feature. You can also click the **Position on Left** command, the **Position on Bottom** command, or the **Position on Right** command to change the Dock position. You can also click **Dock Preferences** to open System Preferences' Dock window.

Add an Icon to the Dock

You can enhance the convenience of the Dock by adding an icon for an application you use frequently. The icon remains in the Dock even when the application is closed, so you can always open the application with a single click.

Add an Icon to the Dock

① Click the **Finder icon** (🖼) in the Dock.

② Click **Applications.**

③ Double-click the icon of the application you want to work with.

● The application's icon appears in the Dock.

④ Ctrl+click or right-click the icon.

⑤ Click **Keep in Dock.**

⑥ Ctrl+click or right-click the icon.

⑦ Click **Quit.**

Your Mac closes the application.

Note: Another way to add an icon to the Dock is to follow Steps 1 and 2, click and drag the application icon, and then drop it inside the Dock.

● The application's icon remains in the Dock.

TIPS

Is there a way to get my Mac to start the application automatically each time I log in to the computer?

Yes, your Mac maintains a list of *login items*, which are applications that run automatically after you log in. You can configure your application as a login item, and your Mac will open it automatically each time you start the machine. Ctrl+click or right-click the application's Dock icon and then click **Open at Login.**

Login Items
✓ Lotus Notes
✓ Illustrator
✓ iView
✓ Photoshop

How do I remove an icon from the Dock?

If the application is currently running, click 🔘 to close the application. Now Ctrl+click or right-click the application's Dock icon and then click **Remove from Dock.** You can remove any Dock icon except Finder (🖥) and Trash (🗑). Note that removing an application's Dock icon does not delete the application itself.

poof!

Hide
the Dock

If you would like more room on
your Mac's screen to display
your applications, you can hide
the Dock to free up some screen
space.

**When the Dock is hidden, it is still
easily accessible whenever you need to
use it.**

TURN ON DOCK HIDING

1. Click .

2. Click **Dock**.

3. Click **Turn Hiding On.**

● Your Mac removes the Dock from
the desktop.

DISPLAY THE DOCK TEMPORARILY

① Move the mouse ▸ to the bottom of the screen.

● Your Mac temporarily displays the Dock.

Note: To hide the Dock again, move the mouse (▸) away from the bottom of the screen.

How do I stop hiding the Dock?

When you no longer need the extra screen space for your applications, you can turn off Dock hiding to bring the Dock back into view. Click 🍎, click **Dock,** and then click **Turn Hiding Off.**

Is there a faster way to hide the Dock?

Yes. You can quickly hide the Dock by pressing Option + ⌘ + D. This keyboard shortcut is a toggle, which means that you can also turn off Dock hiding by pressing Ctrl + F3. When the Dock is hidden, you can display it temporarily by pressing Fn + Ctrl + F3 (on a notebook keyboard, you must press n++).

Add a Widget to the Dashboard

You can make the Dashboard better by customizing it to include any widgets that you find useful or informative.

A *widget* is a mini-application, particularly one designed to perform a single task, such as displaying the weather, showing stock data, or providing sports scores.

Add a Widget to the Dashboard

① Click .

② Click **Applications.**

③ Double-click **Dashboard.**

Your Mac displays the Dashboard and its current set of widgets.

④ Click **Dashboard Plus (⊕).**

Your Mac displays its collection of widgets.

5 Use the arrows (and) to scroll to the widget you want to add.

6 Click the widget.

● Your Mac adds the widget to the Dashboard.

7 Use the mouse ▶ to click and drag the widget to the position you prefer.

● If the widget is configurable, it displays an *i* when you position the mouse ▶ over the widget.

8 Click the *i.*

9 Configure the widget as needed.

10 Click **Done.**

11 Click the desktop.

Your Mac closes the Dashboard.

TIPS

Are there faster methods I can use to open the Dashboard?

The fastest way to start the Dashboard is to click the Dashboard icon ( ) in the Dock. If your hands are on the keyboard, you can also display the Dashboard quickly by pressing F4 . If you have a notebook Mac, press Fn + F4 , instead. Note, too, that you can also press F4 (or Fn + F4) to close the Dashboard.

How do I remove a widget from the Dashboard?

Dashboard gives you a couple of ways to remove widgets. If you just want to remove a single widget, press and hold , position the mouse ▶ over the widget, and then click the Close button ( ) that Dashboard displays in the upper-left corner of the widget. If you want to remove more than one widget, click to display the available widgets, and then click in each widget that you want to remove.

CHAPTER

13

Networking with Your Mac

If you have multiple computers in your home or office, you can set up these computers as a network to share information and equipment. Assuming you already have your computers connected, this chapter shows you how to work with the other computers on your network, and how to share your Mac's resources with other network users.

Understanding Networking

A *network* is a collection of computers that are connected using either a cable hookup or a wireless hookup. A network gives you a number of advantages, such as being able to share files and equipment.

Share Files

Networked computers are connected to each other, and so they can exchange files with each other along the connection. This enables people to share information and to collaborate on projects. Networks also include built-in security, so that you can control what files you share with other people.

Share Equipment

Computers connected over a network can share some types of equipment. For example, one computer can share its printer, which enables other network users to send their documents to that printer. Networked computers can also share hard drives, CD or DVD drives, and document scanners.

Wired Networking

Network Cable

A *network cable* is a special cable designed for exchanging information. One end of the cable plugs into the network port in the back of a computer on the network, and the other end plugs into the network's router, discussed next. Information, shared files, and other network data travel through the network cables.

Router

A *router* is a central connection point for all of the computers on the wired portion of the network. For each computer, you run a network cable from the computer's network port to a port in the back of the router.

When network data travels from computer A to computer B, it first goes out through computer A's network port, along its network cable, and into the router. Then the router passes the data along computer B's network cable and into its network port.

Wireless Networking

Wireless Connections

A wireless network is a collection of two or more computers that communicate with each other using radio signals instead of cable. The most common wireless technology is Wireless Fidelity, which is also called Wi-Fi (rhymes with hi-fi) or 802.11. There are four main types — 802.11, 802.11a, 802.11b, and 802.11g — each of which has its own range and speed limits. (A fifth type — 802.11n — may be available in 2009.)

Wireless Access Point

A wireless access point (AP) is a device that receives and transmits signals from wireless computers to form a wireless network. Many APs also accept wired connections, which enables both wired and wireless computers to form a network. If your network has a broadband modem, you can connect the modem to a type of AP called a *wireless gateway,* which extends Internet access to all of the computers on the network.

Connect to a Wireless Network

If your Mac has built-in wireless networking capabilities, you can use them to connect to a wireless network that is within range. This could be a network in your home, your office, or a public location such as a coffee shop.

Most wireless networks have security turned on, which means you must know the correct password to connect to the network.

Connect to a Wireless Network

1 Click the **AirPort status icon** (📶) in the menu bar.

Note: AirPort is the name that Apple uses for its line of wireless networking devices.

Your Mac locates the wireless networks that are within range of your Mac.

● The available networks appear in the menu.

● Networks with a **Lock icon** (🔒) require a password to join.

2 Click the wireless network you want to join.

If the wireless network is secure, your Mac prompts you for the password.

③ Use the Password text box to type the network password.

● If the password is very long, you can click **Show password** (☐ changes to ☑) to see the actual characters instead of dots. This helps to ensure you type the password correctly.

④ Click **OK.**

Your Mac connects to the wireless network.

● The AirPort status icon changes from 🛜 to 🛜 to indicate the connection.

I know a particular network is within range, but I do not see it in the list. Why not?

Some wireless networks do not broadcast their availability as a security precaution. However, you can still connect to such networks, assuming you know the password if one is required. Click 🛜 and then click **Join Other Network.** Use the Network Name text box to type the name of the network, and use the Security list to click ⬍ and then click the network's security type. Follow Steps **3** and **4** to join the network.

Can I make a wireless connection to another Mac without using an access point?

Yes, you can create what is known as an *ad hoc wireless network.* Click 🛜 and then click **Create Network.** Edit the Name text box, if desired, and then click **Require Password** (☐ changes to ☑). In the Security list, click ⬍ and then click **128-bit WEP.** Use the Password text box to type a 13-character password, and then type it again in the Verify text box. Click **OK.** Your other Mac can now connect to this network.

Connect to a Network Resource

To see what other network users have shared on the network, you can use the Network folder to view the other computers and then connect to them to see their shared resources.

To get full access to a Mac's shared resources, you must connect with a user name and password for an administrator account on that Mac. Note, too, that your Mac can also connect to Windows computers.

Connect to a Network Resource

① Click **Finder** (🖥).

② Click **Go.**

③ Click **Network.**

Note: Another way to run the Network command is to press Shift + ⌘ + K .

The Network folder appears.

● Each icon represents a computer on your local network.

④ Double-click the computer you want to connect to.

Your Mac connects to the network computer using the Guest account.

Note: *The Guest account has only limited access to the network computer and only limited privileges to work with shared resources on that computer.*

5 Click **Connect As.**

Your Mac prompts you to connect to the network computer as a registered user.

6 Use the Name text box to type the username of an account on the network computer.

7 Use the Password text box to type the password of the account.

8 To store the account data, click **Remember this password in my keychain** (☐ changes to ☑).

9 Click **Connect.**

Your Mac connects to the computer and shows the shared resources that you can access.

10 When you are done, click **Disconnect.**

TIPS

Is there a faster way to connect to a network computer?

Yes. If your Mac detects network computers that are sharing resources, it usually displays the names of those

▼ SHARED
🖥 iMac ←●
🖳 Mac mini
💻 MacBook Pro

computers in Finder's sidebar area, under the Shared section. Click the computer you want to connect with and then follow Steps **5** through **9** to connect as a registered user.

● Click the computer you want to connect with.

How can I connect to a computer that does not appear in the Network folder?

If you are sure that the computer is sharing resources on the network, Ctrl-click or right-click 🖳, and then click **Connect to Server.** In the Connect to Server dialog box, use the Server Address text box to type the address: for a Mac, type the Mac's network name followed by **.local;** for a Windows PC, type **smb://** followed by the PC's name; for any computer, type its IP address. Click **Connect.**

Turn On File and Printer Sharing

You can share your files and printers with other network users. This enables those users to access your files and print on your printers over the network. Before you can share these resources, you must turn on your Mac's file- and printer-sharing features.

To learn how to share a particular folder, see "Share a Folder" later in this chapter; to learn how to share a particular printer, see "Share a Printer" later in this chapter.

Turn On File and Printer Sharing

① Click the **Apple icon** (apple).

② Click **System Preferences.**

Note: You can also click ![icon] in the Dock.

The System Preferences window appears.

③ Click **Sharing.**

The Sharing window appears.

④ Click the **File Sharing** check box
(☐ changes to ☑).

*Note: If your Mac is set up to go into sleep mode
after an idle period, a message appears to remind
you of this. Click **OK**.*

You can now share your folders,
as described in the next section.

⑤ Click the **Printer Sharing** check
box (☐ changes to ☑).

You can now share your printers,
as described later in this chapter.

TIPS

**Another user has asked me for my
Mac's IP address. How do I look
that up?**

Your Mac gives you a couple of ways
to do this. Follow Steps **1** to **3** in this
section, click **File Sharing** (click the
name, not the check box); the series of digits
after afp:// is your IP address (such as
192.168.0.61). Alternatively, follow Steps **1** and **2,**
click **Network,** click **Ethernet** (or click **AirPort** if
you have a wireless network connection), and
then read the IP Address value.

**What is the Public folder and how
do I access it?**

Your user account's Public folder is a
special folder that your Mac creates
automatically and that you use to
share files with other people on the
network. If someone connects to your Mac using
your username and password, he or she has full
access to the Public folder. Everyone else can only
read the contents of the folder. To access the
folder, click 📷, click your user name, and then
open the Public folder.

Share a Folder

You can share one of your folders on the network, enabling other network users to view and optionally edit the files you place in that folder.

Your Mac automatically shares your Public folder, but you can share other folders. Sharing a folder enables you to work on a file with other people without having to send them a copy of the file.

Share a Folder

① Click 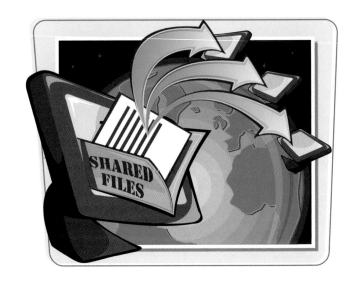.

② Click **System Preferences.**

Note: You can also click 🔲 in the Dock.

The System Preferences window appears.

③ Click **Sharing.**

④ Click **File Sharing**.

*Note: Be sure to click the **File Sharing** text, not the check box. This ensures that you do not accidentally uncheck the check box.*

⑤ Under Shared Folders, click +.

⑥ Click the folder you want to share.

⑦ Click **Add**.

Your Mac begins sharing the folder.

● The folder appears in the Shared Folders list.

⑧ Click the folder.

⑨ For the Everyone user, click the current permission and then click the permission you want to assign.

● The current permission is indicated with a check mark (✓).

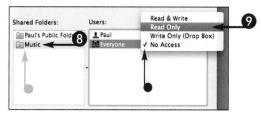

TIPS

What are the differences between the various types of permissions I can assign to users?

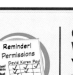

Permissions define what users can and cannot do with the shared folder:

● **Read & Write:** Users can open files, add new files, rename or delete existing files, and edit file contents.

● **Read Only:** Users can open files, but cannot add, delete, rename, or edit files.

● **Write Only (Drop Box):** Users can add files to the folder, but cannot open the folder.

● **No Access:** Users cannot open (or even see) the folder.

Can I share folders with Windows users?

Yes. In the Sharing window, click **Options** and then click the **Share files and folders using SMB** check box (☐ changes to ☑). Click your user account (☐ changes to ☑), use the Password text box to type your account password, click **OK**, and then click **Done**. If you're a Windows user, you must enter your username and password to see your shared folders.

Share a Printer

If you have a printer connected to your Mac, you can share the printer with the network, enabling other network users to send their documents to your printer.

Sharing a printer saves money and time because you only have to purchase and configure one printer for all the computers on your network.

Share a Printer

1 Click .

2 Click **System Preferences.**

Note: You can also click in the Dock.

The System Preferences window appears.

3 Click **Sharing.**

④ Click **Printer Sharing.**

Note: Be sure to click the **Printer Sharing** text, not the check box. This ensures that you do not accidentally uncheck the check box.

⑤ Click the check box beside the printer you want to share (☐ changes to ☑).

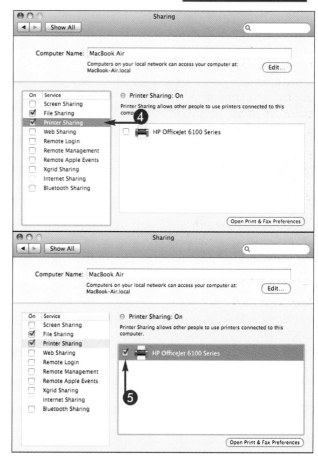

TIP

Is there another method I can use to share a printer?

Yes, you can follow these steps:

① Click .

② Click **System Preferences.**

③ Click **Print & Fax.**

④ Click the printer you want to share.

⑤ Click the **Share this printer** check box (☐ changes to ☑).

Add a Shared Printer

You can send a document from your Mac to a shared printer attached to a network computer. This enables you to use just a single printer for all the computers in your network. Before you can do this, you must add a shared printer to your Mac.

Add a Shared Printer

1 Click .

2 Click **System Preferences.**

Note: You can also click [icon] in the Dock.

The System Preferences window appears.

3 Click **Printer & Fax.**

4 Click +.

5 Click **Default.**

6 Click the shared printer.

● Look for the word *Shared* in the printer description.

7 Click **Add.**

Your Mac adds the printer.

Can I add a shared Windows printer?
Yes, if you have Windows computers on your network you can connect to any printers that they share. Follow Steps **1** to **4** and then click the **Windows** tab. Click the Windows workgroup, click the computer with the shared printer, log on to the Windows computer, and then click the shared printer you want to use. In the Print Using list, click +, click **Select a driver to use,** and then click the printer in the list that appears. Click **Add.**

How do I print to the shared network printer that I added?
In any application that supports printing, click **File** and then click **Print.** You can also press ⌘+P. In the Print dialog box, use the Printer list to click + and then click the shared printer you added in this section. Choose any other printing options you require, and then click **Print.**

Maintaining Your Mac

To keep your Mac running smoothly, maintain top performance, and reduce the risk of computer problems, you need to perform some routine maintenance chores. This chapter shows you how to empty the Trash, delete unnecessary files, update applications, back up your files, and more.

Empty the Trash

When you delete a file, your Mac sends it to the Trash folder. You can free up disk space on your Mac by periodically emptying the Trash folder.

You should empty the Trash folder at least once a month.

Empty the Trash

① Click the **Finder icon** ().

② Click **Finder** from the menu.

③ Click **Empty Trash.**

● You can also `Ctrl`-click or right-click the **Trash icon** (🗑) and then click **Empty Trash.**

Note: *Another way to select the Empty Trash command is to press* `Shift` + `⌘` + `Del`.

Your Mac asks you to confirm.

④ Click **OK.**

Your Mac empties the Trash folder (🗑 changes to 🗑).

Are you sure you want to remove the items in the Trash permanently?

You cannot undo this action.

Cancel   OK

Organize Your Desktop

If you use your Mac's desktop to store files and copies of documents, the desktop can become disarrayed, making it hard to find the icon you want. You can make your desktop easier to navigate by organizing the icons.

Organize Your Desktop

1 **Ctrl**-click or right-click the desktop.

2 Click **Arrange By.**

3 Click **Name.**

● If you just want to nudge each icon into the nearest row and column, click **Clean Up,** instead.

● Your Mac organizes the icons alphabetically and arranges them in rows and columns from right to left.

Check Hard Disk Free Space

If you run out of room on your Mac's hard disk, you will not be able to install more applications or create more documents. To ensure this does not happen, you can check how much free space your hard disk has left.

CHECK FREE SPACE USING FINDER

1 Click 🔲.

2 Click **Macintosh HD.**

3 Read the "available" value, which tells you the amount of free space left on the hard disk.

DISPLAY FREE SPACE ON THE DESKTOP

1 Click the desktop.

2 Click **View.**

3 Click **Show View Options.**

Note: *You can also run the Show View Options command by pressing* ⌘ *+* J *.*

The Desktop dialog box appears.

④ Click **Show item info**
(☐ changes to ☑).

⑤ Click **Close** (●).

● Your Mac displays the amount of
free hard disk space under the
Macintosh HD icon.

How often should I check my Mac's hard disk free space?

With normal computer use, you should check your Mac's hard disk free space about once a month. If you install programs, create large files, or download media frequently, you should probably check your free space every couple of weeks.

What should I do if my Mac's hard disk space is getting low?

First, you should empty the Trash folder, as described earlier in this chapter. Next, you should uninstall any applications that you no longer use, as described in the next section. If you have any documents that you are sure you no longer need — particularly large media files — you should send them to the Trash and then empty the Trash folder.

Uninstall Unused Applications

If you have an application that you no longer use, you can free up some disk space and reduce clutter in the Applications folder by uninstalling that application.

① Click 🖥.

② Click **Applications**.

③ Click the application or its folder.

④ Click and drag the application or its folder and drop it on the **Trash icon** (🗑).

Your Mac uninstalls the application.

TIPS

Is there another way to uninstall an application?

Yes, in some cases. A few Mac applications come with a separate program for uninstalling the application:

① Follow Steps **1** to **3**.

② If the application has its own folder, examine the contents for an icon with "Uninstaller" in the name.

③ Double-click that icon and then follow the instructions on-screen.

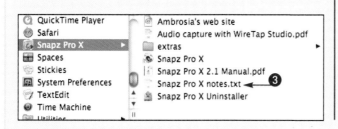

Can I restore an application that I uninstalled accidentally?

If you used the application's uninstall program, the only way to restore the application is to reinstall it. If you sent the application to the Trash, and that was the most recent operation you performed, click 📋, click **Edit,** and then click **Undo Move of "Application"** (where *Application* is the name of the application you want to restore). Otherwise, click 📋, and then use the Trash folder to click and drag the application and drop it on Applications.

Set a Software Update Schedule

Apple makes Mac OS X updates available from time to time. These updates fix problems, add new features, and resolve security issues. You can reduce computer problems and maximize online safety by setting up your Mac to download and install these updates automatically.

By default, your Mac checks for updates every day. You can configure Software Update to check for updates only once a week or once a month.

Set a Software Update Schedule

① Click .

② Click **System Preferences**.

Note: You can also click in the Dock.

The System Preferences window appears.

③ Click **Software Update**.

The Software Update preferences appear.

❹ Click **Scheduled Check.**

❺ Click **Check for updates**
(☐ changes to ☑).

❻ In the **Check for updates**
pop-up menu, click ⬍ and then click the schedule you want: Daily, Weekly, or Monthly.

❼ Click **Download important updates automatically**
(☐ changes to ☑).

Your Mac checks for updates on your selected schedule, and downloads important updates automatically.

Do I have to let my Software Update do the checking automatically?
Technically, no, you do not have to rely on Software Update's automatic checking. Instead, you can check for software updates by hand, as described in "Update Software by Hand". However, this is not a good idea because you should always keep your Mac software up to date, and this might not happen if you try to remember to check for updates yourself.

How does Software Update work?
When the time comes for an update check, Software Update first examines what applications and system software you have installed on your Mac. Then, for each program, Software Update queries an Internet database on Apple's site to see if the program has an update available. If it does, Software Update adds the program to the update list. If the update is considered important, Software Update immediately downloads the update. The Software Update icon then bounces in the Dock to let you know that updates are available.

Update Software by Hand

Your Mac checks for new software updates automatically on a regular schedule. If you turned off this feature or configured it to be less frequent, you can still keep your Mac up to date by checking for updates yourself.

See "Set a Software Update Schedule" to learn how to configure the Software Update schedule.

Update Software by Hand

① Connect to the Internet, if you have not already done so.

② Click [Apple menu].

③ Click **Software Update.**

Your Mac connects with Apple's servers and checks for new updates.

Your Mac displays the list of available updates.

● A description of the selected update appears here.

● If you install any updates that display the Restart icon (⟳), you must restart your Mac to complete the installation.

④ Click the check box for any update you do not want to install (☑ changes to ☐).

⑤ Click **Install X Items** (where X is the number of updates you have selected).

Your Mac asks for the adminstrator password.

6 Use the Password text box to type your password.

7 Click **OK.**

For some updates, your Mac displays a software license agreement.

8 Click **Agree.**

For some updates, your Mac prompts you to restart the computer.

9 If you have any unsaved work, save and close those documents.

10 Click **Restart.**

TIPS

Should I always install every available update?

As a general rule, yes, you should install every available update. However, some exceptions exist. For example, if an update is available for an application that you never use, you can safely skip that update. Also, if your Internet connection is slow, you may prefer to install the updates one at a time.

Is the Mac OS X Update important?

Yes, any update named Mac OS X Update is very important. These are major upgrades to your Mac's operating system, and they generally improve system stability and security. Because such an update affects your entire Mac and is usually quite large — often several hundred megabytes — it is best to install this update on its own.

Remove Unneeded Login Items

If your Mac has login items that you no longer need, those items may slow down your Mac's startup and consume extra system memory. From time to time you should check your user account's login items and remove those you no longer need.

Remove only a login item that you are sure you do not need or that is causing a problem.

① Click .

② Click **System Preferences.**

Note: You can also click ⬚ in the Dock.

The System Preferences window appears.

③ Click **Accounts.**

④ Click the Lock icon (🔒).

⑤ Use the Password text box to type your password.

⑥ Click **OK.**

🔒 changes to 🔓.

⑦ Click **Login Items.**

⑧ Click the item you want to remove.

⑨ Click ⊟.

Your Mac removes the login item.

⑩ Click 🔓 (🔓 changes to 🔒).

What is a login item?

When you start your Mac, many behind-the-scenes tasks get performed to set up the computer for your use. One of these tasks is that your Mac checks the list of items that are supposed to start automatically when you log in to your user account. These items are usually applications, but they can also be files, folders, and shared network locations. These are called *login items*.

Can you give me an example of a problem related to a login item?

Sure. If you uninstall an application by moving it to the Trash as described earlier, the application may leave behind one or more login items, and these will cause an error each time you log in. Similarly, if a login item refers to a folder that no longer exists, you will see an error similar to the one shown here.

Configure Time Machine Backups

Macs are reliable machines, but they do crash and all hard disks eventually die, so at some point your data will be at risk. To avoid losing that data forever, you need to configure your Mac's Time Machine feature to perform regular backups.

To use Time Machine, your Mac requires a second hard disk. This can be a second internal disk, but on most Macs the easiest course is to connect an external hard disk, which is what this task assumes.

Configure Time Machine Backups

1 Connect an external USB or FireWire hard disk to your Mac.

● When your Mac recognizes the external hard disk, it adds an icon for the disk to the desktop.

Your Mac asks if you want to use the hard disk as your backup disk.

2 Click **Use as Backup Disk**.

The Time Machine preferences appear.

● This area shows you information about your backups.

③ Click **Close** ().

Note: To make changes to your backup configuration or to examine backup information, click in the Dock and then click **Time Machine.**

How do Time Machine backups work?

Time Machine makes backing up your Mac easy because it is all handled automatically on the following schedule:

● The initial backup occurs one hour after you configure Time Machine for the first time. This backup includes your entire Mac.

● Time Machine runs another backup every hour. These hourly backups include just those files and folders that you have changed or created since the most recent hourly backup.

● Time Machine runs a daily backup that includes only those files and folders that you have changed or created since the most recent daily backup.

● Time Machine runs a weekly backup that includes only those files and folders that you have changed or created since the most recent weekly backup.

Restore Files Using Time Machine

Because Time Machine makes hourly, daily, and weekly backups, it stores older copies and older versions of your data. You can use these backups to restore any file that you accidentally delete, overwrite, or improperly edit.

Restore Files Using Time Machine

① Click .

② Click the folder you want to restore, or the folder that contains the file you want to restore.

● If you want to restore your entire hard disk, choose **Macintosh HD** in the sidebar.

Note: *Restore your entire hard disk only if your original hard disk crashed and you have had it repaired or replaced.*

③ Click **Time Machine** (⊙).

The Time Machine interface appears.

● Each window represents a backed-up version of the folder.

● This area tells you when the displayed version of the folder was backed up.

● You can use this timeline to navigate the backed-up versions.

④ Navigate to the date that contains the backup version of the folder or file.

5 If you are restoring a file, click the file.

6 Click **Restore.**

If another version of the folder or file already exists, Time Machine asks if you want to keep it or replace it.

7 Click **Replace.**

Time Machine restores the folder or file.

How do I navigate the backups in the Time Machine interface?
Here are the most useful techniques:

- Click the top arrow to jump to the earliest version; click the bottom arrow to return to the most recent version.

- Press and hold the ⌘ key and click the arrows to navigate through the backups one version at a time.

- Use the timeline to click a specific version.

- Click the version windows.

Recondition Your Mac Notebook Battery

To get the most performance out of your Mac notebook's battery, you need to recondition the battery by cycling it. *Cycling* a battery means letting it completely discharge and then fully recharging it again.

To maintain optimal performance, you should cycle your Mac notebook battery once a month or so.

Recondition Your Mac Notebook Battery

DISPLAY THE BATTERY STATUS PERCENTAGE

① Click the **Battery status icon** (⊡).

② Click **Show**.

③ Click **Percentage**.

Your Mac shows the percentage of available battery power remaining.

CYCLE THE BATTERY

① Disconnect your Mac notebook's power cord.

● The Battery Status icon changes from ⊡ to ▣.

② Operate your Mac notebook normally by running applications, working with documents, and so on.

③ As you work, keep your eye on the Battery Status percentage.

When the Battery Status reaches 5%, your Mac warns you that it is now running on reserve power.

④ Click **OK.**

⑤ Reattach the power cord.

Your Mac restarts and the Battery Status icon changes from 🔋 to 🔌.

⑥ Leave your Mac plugged in at least until the Battery Status shows 100%.

I do not see the battery status in my menu bar. How do I display it?

Click 🖥 in the Dock and then click **Energy Saver**. In the Energy Saver window, click **Options** and then click **Show battery status in the menu bar.**

Sleep   Options

☑ Automatically reduce the brightness of the display before display sleep
☐ Restart automatically after a power failure
☑ Show battery status in the menu bar

Do Mac notebooks suffer from the memory effect?

Older portable computers used rechargeable nickel metal hydride (NiMH) or nickel cadmium (NiCad) batteries. The NiMH and NiCad types were phased out because they can suffer from a problem called the *memory effect*, where the battery loses capacity if you repeatedly recharge it without first fully discharging it. All the latest Mac notebooks have rechargeable lithium-ion (Li-ion) batteries. Li-ion batteries are lighter and last longer than NiMH and NiCad batteries and, most importantly, Li-ion batteries do not suffer from the memory effect.

15

Troubleshooting Your Mac

Your Mac is a solid machine, and it should give you many years of dependable performance. However, *all* computers eventually run into problems, and your Mac will likely not be an exception. To help you get through these inevitable rough patches, this chapter offers a few tried-and-true troubleshooting techniques.

Restart Your Mac

If a hardware device is having a problem with some system files, it often helps to restart your Mac. By rebooting the computer, you reload the entire system, which is often enough to solve many computer problems.

For a problem device that does not have its own power switch, restarting your Mac might not resolve the problem because the device remains powered up the whole time. You can power-cycle such devices as a group by power cycling the Mac.

Restart Your Mac

RESTART YOUR MAC

1 Click the **Apple icon** (🍎).

2 Click **Restart.**

Your Mac asks you to confirm.

3 Click **Restart.**

POWER CYCLE YOUR MAC

① Click .

② Click **Shut Down.**

Your Mac asks you to confirm.

③ Click **Shut Down.**

④ Wait 30 seconds to give all devices time to spin down.

⑤ Turn your Mac back on.

TIP

What other basic troubleshooting techniques can I use?

● Make sure that each device is turned on, that cable connections are secure, and that insertable devices (such as USB devices) are properly inserted.

● If a device is battery powered, replace the batteries.

● If a device has an on/off switch, power-cycle the device by turning it off, waiting a few seconds for it to stop spinning, and then turning it back on again.

● Close all running programs.

● Log out of your Mac – click , click **Log Out *User***, where *User* is your Mac user name, and then click **Log Out** – and then log back in again.

When you open System Preferences and click an icon, you may find that some or all of the controls in the resulting preferences window are disabled. To enable those controls, you need to unlock the preferences.

Remember that having locked system preferences is not a glitch. Instead, it is a security feature designed to prevent unauthorized users from making changes to sensitive system settings.

① Click the **System Preferences icon** (⊞) in the Dock.

The System Preferences window appears.

② Click the icon of the system preferences you want to work with (such as Parental Controls, as shown here).

The preferences appear.

③ Click the **System Preferences Locked icon** (🔒).

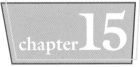

System Preferences prompts you for your Mac's administrator password.

④ Use the Password text box to type your Mac's administrator password.

⑤ Click **OK.**

● 🔒 changes to 🔓.

● Your Mac enables the preferences.

Why should I lock system preferences?

The purpose behind locking system preferences is to prevent unauthorized changes to those preferences. If you are the only person who uses your Mac, then you do not need to worry about this, so you can leave your system preferences unlocked for convenience. However, if other people have access to your Mac, you should probably lock important system preferences by clicking 🔓 (which changes to 🔒).

Is there a way to lock my entire Mac?

Yes, you can configure your Mac to require a password when it wakes up from sleep mode or from the screen saver. Click 🖥 in the Dock, click **Security,** click **General,** and then click **Require password to wake this computer from sleep or screen saver.**

Force a Stuck Program to Close

When you are working with an application, you may find that it becomes unresponsive and you cannot quit the program normally. In that case, you can tell your Mac to force the program to quit.

When you force a program to quit, you lose any unsaved changes in your open documents. Make sure the program really is stuck before forcing it to quit. See the Tip on the following page for more information.

Force a Stuck Program to Close

1 Click .

1 ⮕ 🍎 **iWeb** File Edit Insert Format Arrange View Window Help

2 Click **Force Quit.**

| 🍎 | **iWeb** | File | Edit | Insert | Format | Arrange | View | Window | Help |

About This Mac
Software Update...
Mac OS X Software...

System Preferences...
Dock ▶

Recent Items ▶

2 Force Quit... ⌥⌘⎋

Sleep
Restart...
Shut Down...

Log Out Paul... ⇧⌘Q

The Force Quit Applications
window appears.

③ Click the application you want to
shut down.

④ Click **Force Quit.**

Force Quit Applications

If an application doesn't respond for a while,
select its name and click Force Quit.

🎥 Grab
🎵 iTunes
📷 iWeb
🖼 Finder

You can open this window by pressing
Command+Option+Escape.

Force Quit

Your Mac asks you to confirm that you
want to force the program to quit.

⑤ Click **Force Quit.**

Your Mac shuts down the program.

⑥ Click **Close** (🔘) to close the Force
Quit Applications window.

Do you want to force iWeb to quit?

You will lose any unsaved changes.

Cancel   Force Quit

**Are there easier ways to run the Force
Quit command?**

Yes there are. From the
keyboard, you can run
the Force Quit command
by pressing Option +
⌘ + Option. If the
application has a Dock
icon, press and hold ⌘
and Option and
then click the application's Dock
icon. In the menu that appears, click
Force Quit.

**If an application is not
responding, does that always
mean the program is stuck?**

Not necessarily. For example,
some program operations —
such as recalculating a large
spreadsheet or rendering a 3-D
image — can take minutes, and
during that time the program can appear
stuck. Similarly, your Mac may be low on memory,
which can also cause a program to seem stuck. In this
case, try shutting down some of your other programs
to free up some memory.

Repair a Corrupt Preferences File

One of the most common causes of application flakiness is a preferences file that has somehow become corrupted. You can solve the problem by deleting the preferences file so that the application has to rebuild it.

The downside to this method is that you may have to reconfigure the application's preferences.

Repair a Corrupt Preferences File

① If the problem application is still running, shut it down.

Note: If you have trouble closing the application, see the section "Force a Stuck Program to Close."

② Click **Finder** ().

③ Click your user account folder.

④ Double-click the Library icon.

The Library folder appears.

⑤ Double-click the Preferences icon.

The Preferences folder appears.

6 Click and drag the problem application's preferences file and drop it on the Trash.

Your Mac deletes the preferences file.

7 Run the application and set some preferences.

● The application creates a new preferences file.

What is a preferences file?

A *preferences file* is a document that stores options, settings, and other data related to a particular application. To specify preferences, click the application's name in the menu bar and then click **Preferences.** The application displays a dialog box that you use to specify the preferences. When you are done, the application saves the new settings in the preferences file.

How can I tell which preferences file belongs to the problem application?

Preferences files use the .plist filename extension. In most cases, the filename uses the following general format: com.*company.application*.plist. Here, *company* is the name of the software company that makes the application, and *application* is the name of the program. Here are some examples: com.apple.iTunes.plist; com.microsoft.Word.plist; com.palm.HotSync.plist.

Reset a Forgotten Password

If you forget the password associated with your Mac's main user account, you will be unable to log on to that account and to perform activities such as updating your Mac. You can recover from this problem by resetting the administrative password.

To reset your Mac's administrative password, you need to have the original installation DVD that came with your Mac or that you used to install Mac OS X.

① Insert the Mac OS X Installation DVD.

② Restart your Mac.

③ Press and hold **C** while your Mac is restarting.

*Note: You can release **C** when you see the Apple logo.*

The Mac OS X screen appears.

④ Click the language you want to use.

⑤ Click **Continue** (⊙).

The Mac OS X Installer appears.

⑥ Click **Utilities.**

⑦ Click **Reset Password.**

The Reset Password dialog box appears.

⑧ Click **Macintosh HD.**

⑨ Click the **drop-down list** (◆) and then click your Mac's main user account.

⑩ Type the new password.

⑪ Retype the new password.

⑫ Type a password hint.

⑬ Click **Save.**

⑭ Click **OK.**

⑮ Press ⌘+Q.

Reset Password quits and returns you to Mac OS X Installer.

⑯ Press ⌘+Q.

Installer asks you to confirm you want to quit.

⑰ Click **Restart.**

Your Mac restarts with your new password in effect.

How do I reset passwords for my Mac's other accounts?

Follow these steps:

① Log in to your Mac using the main administrative account.

② Click 🖼 in the Dock.

③ Click **Accounts.**

④ Click 🔒, type your administrative password, and click **OK.**

⑤ Click the user account.

⑥ Click **Reset Password.**

⑦ Type the new password.

⑧ Retype the new password.

⑨ Type a password hint.

⑩ Click **Reset Password.**

Resetting the account password doesn't reset the password for the user's "login" keychain.

To reset the password for the "login" keychain, use Keychain Access, located in the Utilities folder.

New Password: •••••••••• **⑦**

Verify: •••••••••• **⑧**

Password Hint: Mother's maiden name and year of **⑨**
(Recommended) birth

Cancel   Reset Password **⑩**

Repair Disk Permissions

If the permissions on one or more of your Mac's system files become corrupted, your Mac may freeze, run slowly, or become unstable. You can solve these problems by repairing your Mac's disk permissions.

① Click 📷.

② Click **Applications.**

③ Double-click **Utilities.**

Note: You can also open the Utilities folder by pressing Shift + ⌘ + U .

The Utilities folder opens.

④ Double-click **Disk Utility.**

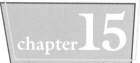

The Disk Utility window appears.

⑤ Click your Mac's hard disk.

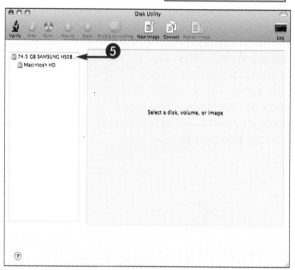

⑥ Click **First Aid.**

⑦ Click **Repair Disk Permissions.**

Your Mac repairs the disk permissions.

⑧ When the repair is complete, press ⌘+Q to quit Disk Utility.

What are disk permissions?

All the files on your Mac have *permissions* applied to them. Permissions are a collection of settings that determine what users or groups of users can do with each file. For example, if a file implements read-only permissions, it means that all users can only read the contents of the file and cannot make any changes to the file or delete it. If the permissions for your Mac's system files change or get corrupted, it can cause all kinds of problems, including program lock-ups and unstable system behavior.

How do I repair permissions if I cannot start my Mac?

Corrupt disk permissions often prevent your Mac from booting. In this case, follow Steps 1 to 6 in the "Reset a Forgotten Password" section, click **Disk Utility,** and then follow Steps 5 to 7 in this section.

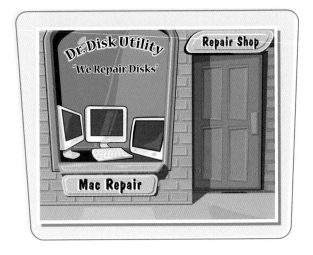

If your Mac will not start, or if an application freezes, an error on the main hard disk is possibly causing the problem. To see if this is the case, you need to repair the hard disk using the Disk Utility program.

To repair your Mac's main hard drive, you need to have the original installation DVD that came with your Mac or that you used to install Mac OS X.

Repair a Disk

1 Insert the Mac OS X Installation DVD.

2 Restart your Mac.

3 Press and hold **C** while your Mac is restarting.

Note: You can release **C** *when you see the Apple logo.*

The Mac OS X screen appears.

4 Click the language you want to use.

5 Click ⊡.

The Mac OS X Installer appears.

6 Click **Utilities.**

7 Click **Disk Utility.**

The Disk Utility window appears.

8 Click your Mac's hard disk.

9 Click **First Aid.**

10 Click **Repair Disk.**

Disk Utility verifies the hard disk and attempts to repair any errors it finds.

● Information on the disk checks appears here.

● The result of the checks appears here.

11 Press ⌘+Q.

Disk Utility quits and returns you to Mac OS X Installer.

12 Press ⌘+Q.

Installer asks you to confirm.

13 Click **Restart.**

How do I repair errors on a secondary hard disk?

If you are working with your Mac's main hard disk, you must boot to the Mac OS X Install DVD to repair that disk. For all other hard disks, however, you can perform the repair without rebooting. Click , click **Applications,** click **Utilities,** and then double-click **Disk Utility.** Click the disk you want to repair, click **First Aid,** and then click **Repair Disk.**

What do I do if Disk Utility finds a problem?

In the best-case scenario, Disk Utility reports either "No repairs were necessary" or "The volume Macintosh HD appears to be OK." Otherwise, Disk Utility attempts to fix any errors it finds. If Disk Utility cannot fix the errors, you must turn to a third-party disk repair application. Two useful tools are DiskWarrior (www.alsoft.com) and TechTool Pro (www.micromat.com).

Reinstall Mac OS X

If worse comes to worst and your Mac will not start or if your system is completely unstable, then you need to reinstall the operating system.

To reinstall Mac OS X, you need to have the original installation DVD that came with your Mac or that you used to install Mac OS X.

Reinstall Mac OS X

① Insert the Mac OS X Installation DVD.

② Restart your Mac.

③ Press and hold **C** while your Mac is restarting.

Note: You can release **C** *when you see the Apple logo.*

The Mac OS X screen appears.

④ Click the language you want to use.

⑤ Click 🔘.

The Mac OS X Installer appears.

⑥ Click **Continue.**

The Software License Agreement dialog box appears.

⑦ Click Continue.

Note: In some versions of the Installer, you click Agree instead, and then skip Step 8.

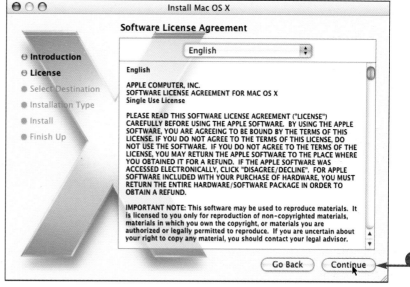

The Installer asks if you agree to the license terms.

⑧ Click Agree.

Under what circumstances should I reinstall Mac OS X?

The most common scenario is when your Mac does not start, and repairing the hard disk as described in the previous section has no effect. Another common scenario is when your Mac suffers from frequent lock-ups, application crashes, and other unstable behavior, and repairing preferences files and disk permissions, as described earlier in this chapter, have no effect.

Do I need to back up my data before reinstalling?

No, this is not usually necessary. The Mac OS X Installer comes with an Archive and Install option that enables you to preserve your Mac's existing user accounts as well as each account's folders. This enables you to use your existing accounts and data with the reinstalled version of OS X. However, this option may be disabled if your Mac does not have enough free hard disk space.

The fastest way to reinstall Mac OS X is to perform the installation using the Archive and Install option. This not only preserves your user accounts and data, but it also bypasses the Setup Assistant, which greatly reduces the number of steps.

The Select a Destination dialog box appears.

9 Click your Mac's main hard disk.

10 Click **Options**.

The installation options appear.

11 Click **Archive and Install** (⊙ changes to ⊙).

12 Click **Preserve Users and Network Settings** (☐ changes to ☑).

13 Click **OK**.

⑭ Click **Continue.**

⑭

⑮ Click **Install.**

Installer reinstalls Mac OS X on your Mac.

⑮

TIPS

Why does my Apple Bluetooth mouse not work with the Installer program?

The Mac OS X Installer application does not come with the necessary device drivers to work with the signals that the Apple Bluetooth mouse or any other wireless mouse generates. You cannot reinstall Mac OS X unless your Mac has a mouse that is physically connected to the computer.

Once Mac OS X is reinstalled, what else do I need to do?

The first thing you should do is update your Mac's software. To do this, click ◉ and then click **Software Update.** Next, you should reinstall any third-party applications that you used on your old Mac OS X installation. Once you have your applications installed, you should check your preferences in each program to make sure they are configured correctly.

Index

Index

Index

Index

Index

Read Less–Learn More®

There's a Visual book
for every learning level...

Simplified

The place to start if you're new to computers. Full color.

- Computers
- Creating Web Pages
- Mac OS
- Office
- Windows

Teach Yourself VISUALLY™

Get beginning to intermediate-level training in a variety of topics. Full color.

- Access
- Bridge
- Chess
- Computers
- Crocheting
- Digital Photography
- Dog training
- Dreamweaver
- Excel
- Flash
- Golf
- Guitar
- Handspinning
- HTML
- Jewelry Making & Beading
- Knitting
- Mac OS
- Office
- Photoshop
- Photoshop Elements
- Piano
- Poker
- PowerPoint
- Quilting
- Scrapbooking
- Sewing
- Windows
- Wireless Networking
- Word

Top 100 Simplified® Tips & Tricks

Tips and techniques to take your skills beyond the basics. Full color.

- Digital Photography
- eBay
- Excel
- Google
- Internet
- Mac OS
- Office
- Photoshop
- Photoshop Elements
- PowerPoint
- Windows

...all designed for visual learners—just like you!